Harvest / Growth and Change / A City in Transit / Naperville /
...ver of Life / Golden Rule Days / Pillars of the Community / Horse Market Days
...the Best That You Can Be / Spirit of the American Doughboy / Yes We Can! /
...lk Visionaries / Volunteers Welcome / The Great Concerto / Veterans' Valor
...d Ham / Mr. and Mrs. Naperville / World's Greatest Artists / Dick Tracy

Century Walk: Art Imitating History

BY JINI LEEDS CLARE

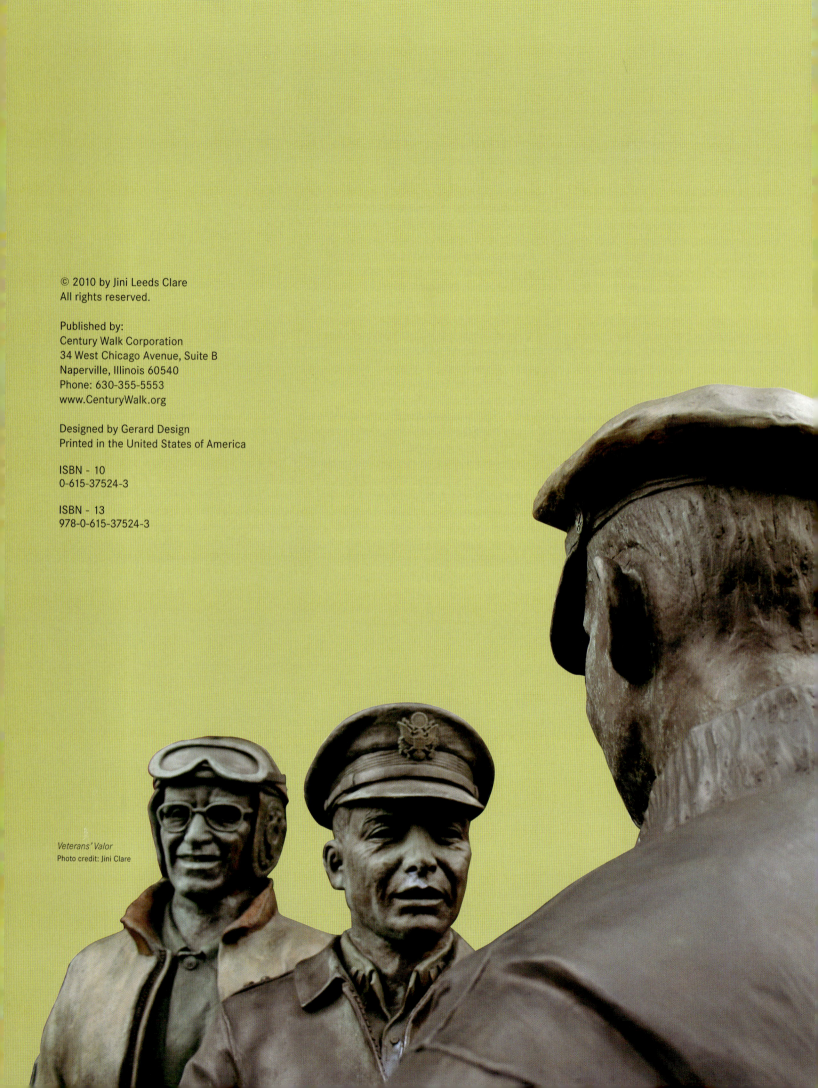

© 2010 by Jini Leeds Clare
All rights reserved.

Published by:
Century Walk Corporation
34 West Chicago Avenue, Suite B
Naperville, Illinois 60540
Phone: 630-355-5553
www.CenturyWalk.org

Designed by Gerard Design
Printed in the United States of America

ISBN - 10
0-615-37524-3

ISBN - 13
978-0-615-37524-3

Veterans' Valor
Photo credit: Jini Clare

Author Jini Clare and her husband, Joe, stand near the *Veterans' Valor* sculpture. The artwork is a tribute to all veterans who have served our nation.

This book is dedicated to my talented parents who gave me a lifetime appreciation for art, to my thoughtful family whose support allowed me to research and write this book, and to the generous community of Naperville that provided the vision and funding for Century Walk.

Parting the Prairie
Photo credit: Don Manderscheid

Table of Contents

The Vision
- 8 Foreword
- 10 Introduction

The Legacy
- 14 *Naperville's Own*
- 16 *The Printed Word*
- 20 *River Reveries*
- 22 *Heartland Harvest*
- 24 *Growth and Change*
- 26 *A City in Transit*
- 28 *Naperville*
- 30 *Man's Search for Knowledge through the Ages*
- 32 *Reading Children*
- 34 *Genevieve*
- 36 *River of Life*
- 38 *Golden Rule Days*
- 40 *Pillars of the Community*
- 44 *Horse Market Days*
- 46 *College, Community and Country*
- 48 *Cars of the Century*
- 50 *A Lifetime Together*
- 52 *Be the Best That You Can Be*
- 54 *Spirit of the American Doughboy*
- 56 *Yes We Can!*
- 58 *Lean on US*
- 60 *Symbiotic Sojourn*
- 62 *Two in a Million*
- 64 *The Way We Were*
- 66 *Riverwalk Visionaries*
- 68 *Volunteers Welcome*
- 70 *The Great Concerto*
- 74 *Veterans' Valor*
- 76 *Parting the Prairie*
- 78 *Officer Friendly*
- 80 *The Cat in the Hat*
- 82 *Green Eggs and Ham*
- 84 *Mr. and Mrs. Naperville*
- 86 *World's Greatest Artists*
- 88 *Dick Tracy*

- 90 Map
- 92 Techniques
- 96 Acknowledgments
- 108 References and Resources

Lean on US
Photo credit: Don Manderscheid

the vision

public art

Chet Rybicki
Mayor of Naperville from 1975 to 1983

"I am so proud of the Riverwalk, Century Walk, and chamber of commerce for keeping our downtown viable. They help attract people to downtown Naperville – not only through the positive atmosphere they help create but also because people have something to do when they are here. A lot of veterans tell me that they are thrilled that Century Walk made it possible for us to have the *Veterans' Valor* sculpture of the five World War II medal winners. Many residents say they have taken their friends to see the sculpture and to show them the kind of respect Naperville shows to its veterans."

"Naperville is fortunate to have residents who recognized the benefits of public art and donated various pieces to the city. Century Walk kept the tradition alive. Today our community enjoys a wide variety of excellent art forms for all to enjoy."

Peg Price
Mayor of Naperville from 1983 to 1991

Mayor A. George Pradel
Mayor of Naperville from 1995 to present

"Through the skills of the artists and the subjects they have chosen, Century Walk motivates us to know the past and moves us into the future of this wonderful community. I am so proud of Naperville for its commitment to public art. Residents and visitors can enjoy dozens of sculptures, mosaics, and murals, and these beautiful works are in public places where people can see them anytime. Century Walk is truly a scenic and inspirational walk down memory lane."

Foreword

By the Century Walk Board of Directors

Century Walk has been a part of Naperville since 1995 — first as a concept and then as a growing canvas of public art throughout the community. Residents have watched the daily progress of artists painting murals on the sides of our downtown buildings. Passersby have stopped to chat with the artists about their works while they were being created. Volunteers have cut tile and placed small pieces in mosaics. Schoolchildren and others have learned Naperville's history through its art.

Century Walk now encompasses 35 pieces of art and has become part of the fabric of the community. This book, *Century Walk: Art Imitating History*, tells the story of this unusual public art project.

While researching the book, the author painstakingly located and interviewed each of the Century Walk artists or their family members. In doing so, Jini Clare learned more about the art, techniques that the artists used, and the impact that art has had on the lives of the artists themselves. While starting out as a book about Century Walk's first 35 pieces, it became more. The book evolved into a story that also shares the importance of art and its influence on the lives of countless individuals.

We encourage you to read about the artworks, the history behind them, and the biographies of the artists. Acknowledgments and a list of the resources that the author used are included at the end of the book for anyone who would like to learn more.

To say that we're very proud of what has been accomplished over these past 15 years would be a gross understatement. Starting only with a borrowed concept, a mission to honor significant people, places, and events of twentieth-century Naperville, and no monies, Century Walk has achieved its goal. As an added benefit, the art that exists today has a replacement value of over $2.5 million, funded evenly by the private and public sectors.

The entire board would like to thank our city council members and other residents for supporting Century Walk throughout the years, and we ask for their continuing support as we move forward in this millennium.

Brand Bobosky first proposed the concept of Century Walk to business and community leaders in 1995. Because of his vision and dedication, this outdoor public art gallery now includes 35 unique pieces of art, including sculptures, murals, and mosaics.

Introduction:
The Vision and the Legacy

Century Walk – a unique outdoor gallery of sculptures, murals, and mosaics – is one Midwestern town's imaginative way of honoring its past while cultivating an appreciation for the visual arts.

Located in Naperville, Illinois, this aesthetic treasure currently features 35 pieces of art. Most of the artwork is on display in the downtown area, encouraging people to walk along the city's tranquil Riverwalk paths and bustling sidewalks to study each piece. Only one, a sculpture at the 95th Street Library, is not within walking distance from the others.

Perpetually on display, with no "admission fee," Century Walk attracts residents and visitors, schoolchildren and teachers, artists and art lovers. It is a source of pride throughout the community. Longtime residents view historic scenes in the murals and share remembrances with their families and friends. Newcomers learn about the people, places, and events during the twentieth century that shaped Naperville into the remarkable town it has become. Students and volunteers proudly point out the contributions that they have made to this creative endeavor.

In a casual outing, visitors can begin their adventure by viewing murals depicting the history of the local news media, the art-deco portrayal of early twentieth-century businesses, and the evolution of transportation. Music lovers might study the visual concerto tracing the story of music in the community, and art enthusiasts can discover the identities of the world's greatest artists. Shoppers may sit on mosaic benches representing those from the old Kroehler Manufacturing Company or feel the *tesserae* on another mosaic that illustrates the story of Naperville's farm families. Children can touch the sculptures of beloved Dr. Seuss characters, learn about early recycling efforts from a bronze fountain, and salute our military heroes.

Inspired by a public mural project that revitalized the small Vancouver Island mill town of Chemainus, British Columbia, Naperville attorney Brand Bobosky first proposed the concept of Century Walk to business and community leaders in 1995. Envisioning a mixture of murals, sculptures, and mosaics, he suggested that the mission of Century Walk would be to honor significant people, places, and events of twentieth-century Naperville. This would complement another of the city's popular landmarks, Naper Settlement, a living-history museum that teaches about the nineteenth century in this pioneering town. It was also believed that the public art project would increase tourism and provide economic benefits locally.

With the support of many organizations and individuals, Century Walk quickly became a reality, and the first three pieces of art were installed in 1996. Throughout the years, the City of Naperville, private donors, civic organizations, businesses, and volunteers have given generously of their money, resources, and time, ensuring the success of Century Walk. A brief description of the history of this public art project and partnerships with the not-for-profit Century Walk Corporation has been written by the Century Walk Board of Directors and is included later in this book.

Today, Century Walk showcases a wide variety of techniques, artistic styles, and media. It is an impressive gallery of art that includes talented Illinois artists as well as internationally renowned artists who have made important contributions to their craft. The works of Century Walk artists are found in the Smithsonian American Art Museum, foreign embassies, and other notable locations throughout the world.

Century Walk – the idea of one visionary man and the gift from a generous community – is truly a legacy for future generations. Join us as we take an artistic stroll through history.

history

Dick Tracy
Photo credit: Jini Clare

the legacy

Relief Sculpture
Size: 7' H x 17' W

Location
On bank building at northeast corner of Washington Street and Jefferson Avenue

Technique
Direct casting

Dedicated
November 3, 1996

Michael Re's original concept for *Naperville's Own* is shown in this drawing.

#1
Naperville's Own
By S. Michael Re

Photo credit: Robert McKendrick

THE ARTIST

S. Michael Re, Sculptor – Born in Chicago in 1950, S. Michael Re studied engineering at the Illinois Institute of Technology for three years before entering the field of commercial art. He credits much of his professional education to his work with master Egyptian sculptor Mustafa Naguib. A former royal sculptor, Naguib had immigrated to the United States and opened a series of sculpture schools in the region – first in Beverly Shores, Indiana, later in Glen Ellyn, Illinois, and ultimately in Chicago. It was at the Naguib School of Sculpture in Glen Ellyn that Re first met the accomplished artist and learned classical techniques of sculpting. Re not only completed the master of sculpture program offered at the school, but he also remained with the renowned sculptor as his assistant until the school closed.

Later, Re opened his own studio in Roselle, specializing in sculpture and marquetry. His pictures – featuring wildlife, landscapes, and Olympic athletes – are made of pieces of wood veneer with many different colors and grain patterns. Re is also well known throughout the area for his skill at making large molds for other artists and foundries. He made the molds for the Michael Jordan sculpture at the United Center and Harry Caray's sculpture at Wrigley Field.

In his artist's statement, Re writes, "All my life I have felt a need to express my observations and feelings through the visual arts. This compulsion has been nourished by the outstanding cultural assets found in Chicago and the surrounding communities. The architecture, public art, galleries, and museums with their incredible wealth of historic and contemporary art are a true local treasure. This cultural environment has over the years attracted, developed, and sustained a large number of talented and acclaimed artists. My opportunities to learn the techniques of art and to develop my talent were greatly enhanced by this community of artists and craftsmen."

The artist first created the 17-foot-wide sculpture in clay. Details of the old bandstand "gazebo," band members, and their instruments can be seen in these pictures.

Naperville's Own

In the first sculpture created for Century Walk's public art project, artist S. Michael Re pays tribute to the important role the Naperville Municipal Band has played in the community for 150 years.

Six musicians – playing a snare drum, French horn, piccolo, sousaphone, coronet, and tenor saxophone – march through time, beginning near the old bandstand "gazebo" that was used for performances from the 1890s until 1926 and moving toward a newer band shell that was home to the popular Central Park concerts from 1966 until 1999. Scenes from those early settings are subtly carved into the sculpture at each end of the relief. While the uniforms of the six large figures do not represent any one period of time during the band's history, they do contain a blend of elements from uniforms over the years. The band members themselves reflect the eventual inclusion of women in a once all-male troupe.

To create this realistic figurative piece, Re began with a detailed drawing and then made a small clay model known as a maquette. He later set up a temporary studio in a friend's local trucking garage, building a vertical wall on which he could apply and sculpt the clay in the same position that the final sculpture would be viewed. Strong armature held the oil-based clay in place and prevented it from falling off the wall as the artist formed, carved, and smoothed the images. Re fabricated the ribbon at the bottom of the sculpture out of plaster.

The artist made the production mold by first measuring and mixing together the components of polyurethane rubber. He then carefully applied the smooth, sticky paste to the clay sculpture with brushes and a trowel, capturing every detail of the surface. After the rubber cured and formed a firm but flexible skin over the clay original, Re covered the rubber with a shell of plaster, called the mother mold. Designed to support and align the flexible rubber sections of the mold while they were being filled, the mother mold was easily separated from the rubber after the sculpture was cast. Ultimately, the rubber skin was carefully peeled away from the sculpture. The surface was finished, patinas were applied, and the lovely relief was installed.

Although *Naperville's Own* appears to be a bronze sculpture, the finished artwork was actually fashioned from an intricate blend of gypsum cement, powdered resins, glass fiber, and polymers. Bronze powder was added to the mix for the main portion of the sculpture. Dune sand and pigments were added to the ribbon section to give it a carved-stone appearance.

Re titled the piece *Naperville's Own* to reflect the historic significance of this local band. The United States Marine Band, founded in 1798 by an Act of Congress, is America's oldest continuously active professional musical organization and is known as "The President's Own."

Murals
Size: *The Printed Word,* First Edition
18' H x 28' W

Location
The former Naperville Sun Building,
9 West Jackson Avenue

Technique
Trompe l'oeil images and detailed portraits, air brushed on prepared and primed brick walls

Dedicated
November 3, 1996

#2

The Printed Word
By Timm Etters

Timm Etters used a scissor lift to reach portions of his murals.

The Printed Word, First Edition

Photo credit: Charles Schabes

THE ARTIST

Photo credit: Charles Schabes

Timm Etters, Muralist – For as long as he can remember, Timm Etters knew that he would become an artist. Born in Elgin, Illinois, in 1968, he believes that his art career began as soon as he could hold a pencil. He drew on whatever he could find: napkins, scratch paper, and even walls. His talent was so striking that his third-grade teacher challenged him with art assignments and included him as a subject in her master's thesis. Although he was diagnosed with color blindness, the young boy continued drawing. By the fifth grade, Timm won his first art contest with the creation of an energy awareness poster for a local company.

The style and direction of Timm's art changed dramatically during the summer before his sophomore year in high school. He became captivated by the hip hop movement, the original culture that celebrated various forms of artistic expression as a way of preventing gang warfare on the streets of New York. The teen embraced the entire culture: the music, the break dancing, the message, and the graffiti art. With a can of spray paint, he soon began to transform weathered walls and rusty bridges into works of art. His graffiti, although illegal, expressed positive messages and inspired those who viewed it.

Continued >

The Printed Word

Originally air brushed on the side of the Naperville Sun Building, *The Printed Word* depicts the history of publishing in Naperville. The artist, Timm Etters, was handpicked to create the mural because he had already completed numerous eye-catching scenes in schools throughout the community. Unfortunately, the artwork was torn down when the building was later sold and remodeled. Etters subsequently agreed to paint a similar piece at another location. The original building owner agreed to finance a new mural, and the "second edition" of *The Printed Word* was dedicated in 1998. Luckily, Etters had a photojournalist document the creation of *The Printed Word* in 1996, and these photos allow us to tell the story of both pieces.

The original mural was designed to show a timeline progressing from the bottom to the top. It begins with one of the first Naperville newspaper publishers and ends as a desktop publishing composition on a computer screen. The first portrait, seen at the bottom left of the mural, is of David Givler, the publisher of the *Naperville Clarion*. Givler, a self-educated man and Civil War veteran who had once marched with Sherman through Georgia, purchased the *DuPage County Press* in 1868 and changed its name. The text written next to Givler's portrait appears in old typewriter font because the first functional typewriters were patented around that time.

At the lower center of the mural is a portrait of Naperville author and publisher James Nichols I. Orphaned at the age of eight and brutalized in a succession of temporary homes, a determined Nichols came to Naperville in 1876 and within a few years became a professor of business at North Western College, now North Central College. Nichols started his own publishing company, J. L. Nichols and Co., and published many books, including *The Business Guide,* which sold over 4,000,000 copies. Although he died young, Nichols had become a wealthy man. He willed $10,000 to the city of Naperville for the establishment of a public library and made other significant contributions enhancing the growth of this community. The text above Nichols' portrait appears as handwritten calligraphy, similar to the notes written by this publishing pioneer.

A portrait of Harold Moser, the 1935 founder and publisher of the *Naperville Sun*, is positioned in the upper left center of the mural. The young Moser, who would eventually become a successful developer and builder in Naperville, hired Harold White Jr. to be the paper's editor. During August of 1936, Harold White and a business partner purchased the growing newspaper. Within two years, White and his bride, Eva, began their lifelong partnership as a journalistic team, working together to publish the *Naperville Sun*. In the mural, the couple is shown setting type on the company's first Linotype machine in 1940. The font above their portrait represents the cleaner type of the new technology. Etters illustrates the link between Moser and the Whites with the nameplate of the newspaper joining their portraits together.

Other local newspapers are depicted in the mural, several as regional papers identified on a drop-down menu on the computer. The desktop publishing page is set within the frame of architectural stonework and overlays a colorful sky. As the history unfolds from past to present, Etters represents the years to come in the background, through images of outer space. The shooting star symbolizes future publishers who are dreaming of someday starting their own publishing companies.

The "second edition" of *The Printed Word* embodies the same people and many of the same images as the first. However, because the wall is wider and almost twice as large as the original brick canvas, the timeline is horizontal rather than vertical. The peeled corner, a trademark of Etters' work, symbolizes turning the page on the present day and taking a peek into the future. That is where the shooting star is revealed. A careful eye will also notice a newspaper draped over the edge of the mural, with its headline stating that *The Printed Word* has a new home.

Murals
Size: *The Printed Word,* Second Edition
15' H x 50' W

Location
Southwest corner of Main Street and Van Buren Avenue

Technique
Trompe l'oeil images and detailed portraits, air brushed on prepared and primed brick walls

Dedicated
November 1, 1998

The Printed Word (Continued)

The Printed Word, Second Edition

Photo credit: Timm Etters

The artist hinted at the loss of the first *The Printed Word* mural by painting this folded newspaper image near the lower edge of the mural. It states, "Mural finds new home."

Photo credit: Jini Clare

THE ARTIST

Timm Etters, Muralist *(continued)* — Timm's active high school life came to a screeching halt in 1985, and his inspirational story began. At sixteen, the young man was diagnosed with the life-threatening disease, testicular cancer. While recovering in his hospital room after surgery, he began searching for purpose and direction in his life as a cancer survivor. The rap lyrics from Grandmaster Melle Mel and the Furious Five's "Beat Street" repeated constantly in his mind:

"Well, a picture can express a thousand words / To describe all the beauty of life you give
And if the world was yours to do over / I know you'd paint a better place to live
Where the colors would swirl / And the boys and girls can grow in peace and harmony
And where murals stand on walls so grand / As far as the eyes are able to see, ha
I never knew art till I saw your face
And there'll never be one to take your place
Cause each and every time you touch a spraypaint can
Michaelangelo's [sic] soul controls your hands…"

At that moment, Timm began to lay out the groundwork that would become the foundation of his company. He even used the money sent to him in get-well cards to purchase his first airbrush. To this day, Etters says, "I look at the experience of hip hop and those days in the hospital to be the biggest, most powerful blessings I've ever had."

The intervention of a police officer who recognized Etters' talents on a spray-painted bridge led to a community service project at the teen's high school. There, under the watchful and gratified eyes of the school principal, Etters painted his first "legal" mural. Today, more than 275 commissioned murals by this talented artist inspire students at over 135 Chicagoland schools. More than 60 of those murals are in Naperville. Etters welcomes classes and small groups to stop by and visit with him in the schools as he moves through the creative process. He teaches students through his artist-in-residence program, offers students positive messages for dealing with adversity, and inspires them to follow their dreams.

David Givler, James Nichols I, Harold Moser, and Harold and Eva White were all important figures in bringing the printed word to people in Naperville during the nineteenth and twentieth centuries.

Below right: Timm Etters carefully painted the portrait of James Nichols I while keeping the publisher's photograph nearby as a reference.

Tile Mosaic Benches
Size: 30" H x 6' L x 30" W

Location
Just east of the shops at 175 West Jackson Avenue, across from the Riverwalk's Dandelion Fountain

Technique
Gluing and grouting tile and glass tessarae onto poured concrete benches

Dedicated
November 3, 1996

#3
River Reveries
By Jennifer Hereth
Assisted by Peter Young

Two fish and a turtle seem to be swimming just below the surface of the water in this *River Reveries* scene.

Photo credit: Jini Clare

Photo credit: Robert McKendrick

THE ARTIST

Jennifer Hereth, Painter and mosaic artist – Chicago artist Jennifer Hereth earned both a BFA and MFA from the School of the Art Institute of Chicago, as well as a certificate in fresco from the Accademia Caerite in Italy. A tenured professor and chair of the Painting Department at the College of DuPage, she has taught painting at the School of the Art Institute of Chicago for 17 years and has been a visiting lecturer at the University of Creation Spirituality under theologian Matthew Fox in Oakland, California, for the past ten years.

Born in Lansing, Michigan, in 1956, Hereth has traveled to many areas of the world to learn about fine art and temporary art rituals in other cultures. She has taught in Egypt, Costa Rica, Mexico, and Brazil and has exhibited her works in North and South America, including a solo exhibition at the Museum of Contemporary Art in São Paulo, Brazil.

Hereth is an expert on *tapates*, the little-known indigenous art form from Guatemala and Brazil. *Tapates* are temporary carpets made out of brightly dyed sawdust. They are created by community members and are traditionally used as part of Easter and Corpus Christi celebrations. Hereth, her assistant, and community members created a *tapate* around the Kroehler lounges for the final dedication of *River Reveries* in October of 1997.

River Reveries

Painter/mosaic artist Jennifer Hereth captures winter and spring scenes along the DuPage River on a special canvas that is uniquely Naperville. The canvas – a pair of Kroehler lounges cast in concrete – is covered with hand-painted and other colorful tiles and mirrors from around the world.

The lounges are reminiscent of a popular sofa made by the Kroehler Manufacturing Company, one of Naperville's largest employers during the last century. Originally named the Naperville Lounge Factory, the manufacturer was the world's largest producer of upholstered furniture and an important part of the local economy from the late 1800s until the plant closed in 1978.

The hand-painted tiles on the first lounge illustrate two women ice skating on the frozen river over 100 years ago. Their skate marks are clearly visible on the ice, and patches of snow frame their small, natural rink. The second lounge features two fishermen sporting their skills at Burlington Dam the following spring. As a pole touches the water, concentric rings spread out across the surface, and bubbles emerge from below. On both lounges, fish and turtles swim in a river that is teeming with life.

The remaining tiles create the ambience of a homemade quilt – reflecting the care that goes into the selection of each piece of fabric in a quilt – as well as the warmth of the upholstered Kroehler lounges. Hand painted by the artist, gathered while teaching in other countries, donated by community members, or scavenged from local thrift stores, each tile brings a unique story to the benches. Inspired by the mosaics of Spanish architect Antoni Gaudí, Hereth deliberately collected an array of broken ceramics and brought the unmatched pieces together in a composition of color and pattern. A peach from a treasured plate, broken by her four-year-old son, has a special place on one of the benches. Mirrors from Brazil add sparkle. Small Italian tiles provide vibrant color, and sarcophagus eyes focus on traditions from Hereth's Egyptian travels.

As young children crawl up on the lounges to play or weary shoppers sit on the benches to rest, *River Reveries* offers them a glimpse of Naperville's past. The mosaic teaches us all about a simpler time along the river.

Jennifer Hereth and her assistant, Peter Young, cement small pieces of tile, called *tesserae*, onto one of the mosaic benches in the top photo. (This photo was reprinted by permission of the *Daily Herald*, Arlington Heights, IL.)

The finished mosaic in the lower photo captures two women skating on the frozen DuPage River. The tiles were hand painted by the artist and recall a once-popular activity that has almost been forgotten.

Tile Mosaic
Size: 6' 3" H at its peak,
3' H at each end x 11' W

Location
Northwest corner of Main Street
and Jefferson Avenue

Dedicated
October 19, 1997

#4

Heartland Harvest

By Kathleen Farrell and
Kathleen Scarboro

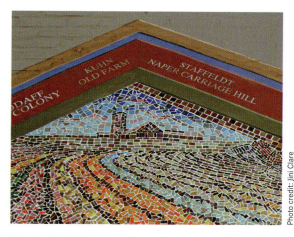

The *Heartland Harvest* mosaic pays homage to the farm families and crops that played such an important role in the development of Naperville. The farm and silo in the distance offer a backdrop to the sweeping fields of grain.

Photo credit: Robert McKendrick

THE ARTISTS

Kathleen Farrell, Painter, sculptor, and mosaic artist – Born in Chicago in 1940, Kathleen Farrell earned a Bachelor of Arts in painting from Southern Illinois University, a master's degree in cultural anthropology from Governors State University, and a Master of Fine Arts in printmaking from L'École Nationale Supérieure des Arts Décoratifs in Paris. An accomplished painter, sculptor, and mosaicist, she founded the Friends of Community Public Art in Joliet in 1996. The organization's goal is to create, plan, promote, and preserve public art and to increase the awareness of Joliet's rich historical and cultural heritage. Farrell was instrumental in helping to establish Century Walk's structure and hire several of its early artists. Farrell was the organization's first administrator.

Kathleen Scarboro, Painter, mosaic artist, and sculptor – Kathleen Scarboro has collaborated with Kathleen Farrell since they first met in France while studying art. Born in Chicago in 1950, Scarboro earned a Bachelor of Arts in painting from Southern Illinois University and a Master of Fine Arts in printmaking from L'École Nationale Supérieure des Beaux-Arts in Paris. A world traveler, she enjoys studying different cultures and painting subjects from life in India and other locales. She works as a muralist, sculptor, and mosaicist with Friends of Community Public Art in Joliet.

Artists Kathleen Farrell (left) and Kathleen Scarboro – (This photo was reprinted by permission of the *Daily Herald*, Arlington Heights, IL.)

Destruction caused by the velvetbean caterpillar is evident in the damaged leaf in the upper photograph, while a colorful butterfly flutters in the harvest fields in the lower photo.

Heartland Harvest

The richness of Naperville's farming history is reflected in this colorful, detailed mosaic entitled *Heartland Harvest*. Designed by artists Kathleen Farrell and Kathleen Scarboro and created with the help of more than 25 community volunteers, this 80-square-foot artwork pays homage to the farm families and crops that played such an important role in the development of this community.

The soybean, oat, wheat, barley, alfalfa, and corn-filled landscapes that once dominated the local scene are depicted with small pieces of Italian glass tile. Rows of crops sweep across the composition in curving diagonal lines, leading to the distant Boecker Granary at the peak of the mosaic. Variegated butterflies dance in the autumn sun, while a destructive velvetbean caterpillar makes its presence known.

To create the mosaic, Scarboro first painted a smaller version of the scene. The artists later projected the intricate design onto a large sheet of paper in their studio and taped sections of the new drawing to sheets of two-inch Styrofoam. They then installed clear contact paper, sticky side up, over the drawings. Volunteers worked in shifts to help the mosaic artists cut 3/4-inch glass tiles into smaller pieces and lay the tesserae carefully into the composition according to color and pattern. When all the tiles were in place, strong clear tape was placed over the completed mosaic. Once on-site, the backing contact paper was removed. A professional tile setter installed the mosaic on the prepared exterior wall of the downtown building and grouted the finished work of art.

The artists outlined the mosaic's barn-like shape with a painted border containing the names of many of the original farms and the subdivisions which they eventually became.

Sculpture
Size: 10' 6" H x 8' W, 2400 pounds

Location
Front courtyard of the Jefferson Hill Shops
at 43 East Jefferson Avenue

Technique
Rolled steel forms with antique tools
welded to surfaces

Dedicated
October 19, 1997

#5

Growth and Change
By Jack Holme

Photo credit: Don Manderscheid

THE ARTIST

Jack Holme, Sculptor — Sculptor Jack Holme was born in Vancouver, British Columbia, in 1923. He received a Bachelor of Science degree in mechanical engineering from the University of British Columbia in 1950 and a master's degree in product design from the Illinois Institute of Technology Institute of Design in Chicago two years later. After graduate study, while earning a living in the business world, his interests turned to photography and jewelry making. In 1967, he discovered Henry Moore's sculpture. "It was then that I was inspired to create my own work," Holme admits. "I was intrigued by the size, shape, and texture of Moore's pieces." Holme began by sculpting small, abstract bronze pieces and later experimented with larger fiberglass works, as well as welded and steel pieces. He sometimes twisted branches, twigs, and discarded metal to create unusual shapes and sculptures. In 1983, he took an early retirement from his 31-year career as an industrial engineer, product developer, and marketer to devote his life to sculpting.

A longtime resident of Darien, Illinois, the artist has shown his works in numerous solo and group sculpture exhibitions and has earned various awards. He has secured corporate and private commissions throughout the United States and Canada. Several of Holme's pieces are on display at the National University of Health Sciences, formerly known as the National College of Chiropractic, in Lombard, Illinois. (The artist's photo was reprinted by permission of the *Daily Herald*, Arlington Heights, IL.)

Local farm families and longtime residents donated the antique tools that are part of this sculpture. The utensils, tools, and other implements were once used in homes, on farms, and in businesses.

Growth and Change

In this sculpture linking Naperville's present to its past, Jack Holme's concept was to create a small museum honoring the strong foundation that pioneers laid down in this community. Children and adults could step inside and learn about the variety of tools local people used during the early 1900s and the contributions they made to the development of this city.

Three rust-colored, gently curved steel sections represent residents, farm families, and business people, welded together, working in harmony to create a strong and independent Naperville. Through the generosity of local farm families and others, the artist obtained antique kitchen utensils, woodworking tools, drills, hammers, saws, and farm implements. Railroad spikes were also donated, highlighting the role of trains in the development and growth of the town. The steel sculpture was fabricated by a foundry in Wheeling, Illinois, using the artist's scale model. The sculptor then welded these once-familiar pieces onto the structure.

Holme envisioned families exploring this sculpture together and grandparents telling younger generations, "These are the things I remember as a child."

Mural
Size: 30' H x 50' W

Location
Southwest corner of Washington Street and Chicago Avenue, on east side of The Lantern building

Technique
Dynamic symmetry combined with *trompe l'oeil* elements, hand painted with acrylic paints

Dedicated
October 19, 1997

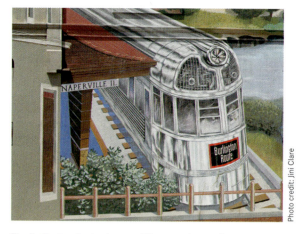

The Burlington Zephyr is one of the many forms of transportation showcased in this dramatic mural.

#6

A City in Transit

By Hector Duarte and Mariah de Forest

Photo credit: Jini Clare

26

THE ARTISTS

Hector Duarte, Muralist — Hector Duarte was born in Caurio, Michoacán, Mexico in 1952, and first visited the United States while attending a mural conference in Chicago in 1978. He was greatly influenced by the works of David Alfaro Siqueiros, one of the great Mexican masters of the Mexican Mural Renaissance. Duarte studied mural painting at the workshop of Siqueiros in 1977. Since moving to Chicago in 1985, Duarte has participated in the creation of more than 50 murals. He has exhibited his paintings and prints at the National Museum of Mexican Art, the School of the Art Institute, the State of Illinois Gallery, the Chicago Historical Society, and Casa Estudio Museo Diego Rivera in Mexico. He has also received numerous awards, including a 2008 Artist Fellowship Award from the Illinois Arts Council, 2005 and 2007 Artistic Production Awards from the Secretary of Culture of the state of Michaocán, and a 1995 Chicago Bar Association Award for best work of public art. In 2006, Duarte participated in the Smithsonian Folklife Festival on the National Mall in Washington, D.C., as an invited muralist. He frequently works out of his studio in Chicago, although his mural work takes him on location throughout Illinois and Mexico. Duarte is cofounder of the Mexican Printmaking Workshop in Chicago and dedicates much of his time teaching mural painting to young people.

Mariah de Forest, Muralist and painter — Mariah de Forest was born in Hinsdale, Illinois, in 1948, and grew up there and on a small farm in Downers Grove. As a child, she was also familiar with Naperville, having spent many summer days swimming in the local quarry, Centennial Beach. She was keenly aware of the importance of the Burlington line to the small western suburbs of Chicago and affectionately gave it a prominent place in *A City in Transit*. De Forest attended the University of Pennsylvania and Mills College in California, where she obtained a Bachelor of Arts in philosophy, painting, and art history. She later earned a Master of Arts degree in painting and art history at Hunter College in New York. Professionally, de Forest taught art history at the University of Illinois, Xavier College, and Northern Illinois University, as well as painting at the Illinois Institute of Technology. This talented artist does numerous commissions, portraits, and murals and has collaborated on several pieces with Hector Duarte. Together they won the 1995 Chicago Bar Association Award for the best work of public art, a 20' x 430' mural named *Lotería*. De Forest works out of her studio in Evanston.

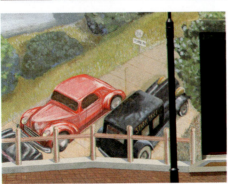

Many of Naperville's early car dealers are represented in *A City in Transit*. Viewers can also discover several makes and models of twentieth-century automobiles in this bird's-eye view of the town.

A City in Transit

The evolution of transportation in Naperville is depicted in *A City in Transit*, a panoramic mural designed from a bird's-eye view, looking down onto the life of this community. Water, train, automobile, and airplane are all intertwined in the circular composition, created with strong diagonal lines that give the piece its dramatic perspective.

Careful study reveals many of the town's early car dealers. Feldott and Flemming, Burgess Motors, Brummel Motor Company, Cromer Motor Company, Clyde Netzley Garage, and Ridley Chrysler-Plymouth are clustered around a bend in the DuPage River. Lee Nelson's Service Station is nearby, and an old buggy seems abandoned outside the DuPage Garage Company. While a man rides his bike, cars of every vintage drive along the streets. One dirt road is identified as "Plank Road/34." Two bridges provide access across the river – the Main Street stone bridge and the Washington Street wooden bridge, where a woman is enjoying a casual stroll. Across town, the Burlington Zephyr comes to a stop at the Naperville train station, and six planes from the Lima Lima Flight Team soar overhead. Adding to the historical setting, the artists include the Pre-Emption House, the Naperville Creamery, and Prince Castles Ice Cream shop to the scene. The steeple of Saints Peter and Paul Church pierces the farming landscape that defined Naperville during the last century.

Designed and painted by Hector Duarte and Mariah de Forest, the mural is an extraordinary example of the concept of dynamic symmetry, a technique that began with the great Mexican muralist David Siqueiros. In accordance with this master's theory, not only is the mural composed of the features of the wall itself, but the composition also takes into account the movements and perspectives of the viewer. The artists also created a stage effect, with *trompe l'oeil* sections of the Lantern Building easing the spectator into the mural on the right and left sides and a fence at the bottom preventing the viewer from "falling into" the painting.

Bronze Relief Map
Size: 12' 11" H x 12' 11" W

Location
Southeast corner of Nichols Library, near the intersection of Jackson Avenue and Webster Street

Technique
Bronze cast in original positive mold

Dedicated
June 22, 1986 and November 1, 1998

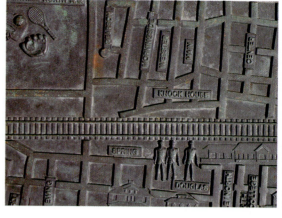

Parks, neighborhood schools, train tracks, and city streets are all represented in this unique map of Naperville.

#7
Naperville
By Gregg LeFevre

Photo credit: Robert McKendrick

THE ARTIST

Photo courtesy of Gregg LeFevre

Gregg LeFevre, Sculptor – Born in Buffalo, New York, in 1946, Gregg LeFevre is renowned for his bronze sculptures, which have been installed in major cities throughout the United States. This self-taught artist has completed over 250 large-scale public commissions, many of them similar to the bronze map he created for Naperville. While these sculptures enhance the daily walks of many city dwellers, they also bring people together to explore the forgotten stories and events that make their own communities unique.

LeFevre's largest project to date is a series of 100 bronze panels embedded in the sidewalks of 41st Street across from the New York Public Library's main building in Manhattan. The two-block-long sculpture contains illustrated quotes about literature. In addition, he created the panels in Union Square which tell the story of that historic gathering place. Also of note are the Literary Walk in Iowa City, the terrazzo flight map on the floor of Terminal D at McCarran International Airport in Las Vegas, and *Boston Bricks* – a sculpture made up of 100 reliefs detailing various aspects of Boston. His works have been favorably reviewed in the *New York Times, Washington Post, Chicago Tribune, Miami Herald, Boston Globe*, and many other publications. He won the Excellence in Design Award from the New York City Arts Commission and has received a number of other grants and awards.

This whimsical map of Naperville captures various neighborhoods, the never-built "Dragon Lake," footsteps in a forest preserve, and the tragic train wreck of 1946.

Photo credit: Jini Clare

Photo credit: Jini Clare

Photo credit: Jini Clare

Naperville

Naperville's history is whimsically portrayed on the bronze map embedded in the sidewalk, just footsteps from Nichols Library. Termed "creative cartography" by artist Gregg LeFevre, this unusual relief sculpture is made up of 36 bronze squares that capture many of the streets, homes, and events that are part of the community's heritage. LeFevre has created a puzzle for onlookers as they search the topographical map for familiar landmarks, activities, and almost-forgotten stories of Naperville's past.

A Conestoga wagon at Naper Settlement, a dragon at the never built "Dragon Lake," planks on old Plank Road, and a jumble of railroad cars strewn across the tracks hint at local history. There are familiar scenes of daily life – families biking, joggers running, pet owners walking their dogs. A catcher's mitt and baseball rest on a playing field, and a family of ducks paddles across Centennial Beach. Tiny bare feet walk through a forest preserve, while birds gather on a branch and watch over their sanctuary. The maze of streets and subdivisions captures Naperville at a moment in time when the town was small and its farm fields were undeveloped.

The piece was donated to the library by Harold and Margaret Moser. A developer once credited with building half of Naperville's homes, Harold Moser played a major role in the growth of Naperville and changing its streetscape. The artwork was first dedicated in 1986. It was one of three privately funded library pieces that became an official part of Century Walk in 1998.

Bas-relief mural
Size: 7' 10" H x 46' 6" W x 13" D

Location
Northeast corner of Nichols Library, near the intersection of Jefferson Avenue and Webster Street

Technique
Brick relief sculpture

Dedicated
April 12, 1987 and November 1, 1998

The trumpeters and drummers carved in this brick sculpture represent the parades that have passed by the library for many years.

#8

Man's Search for Knowledge through the Ages

By Mara Smith
Assisted by Kris King

Photo credit: Robert McKendrick

THE ARTIST

Mara Smith, Brick sculptor – An ancient art first perfected in the friezes of Mesopotamia over 3,000 years ago, brick sculpture became a rare form of expression during the last century. Today, only a dozen or so artists in America carve brick full time. Mara Smith, the creator of *Man's Search for Knowledge through the Ages*, has played a key role in the recent renaissance of this art form. She has been described as "The pioneer of modern brick sculpture."

Born in Houston, Texas, in 1945, Smith earned a Master of Fine Arts degree in ceramic sculpture and metal smithing from Texas Woman's University and North Texas University. While still a student, she was selected to create a series of brick murals to adorn the new Anatole Hotel in Dallas. That commission changed her life – launching her career, catapulting her to fame, and connecting her to the ancient civilizations that inspired her. "I had seen the carved gates of Babylon in history books," she explains. "That I could carve in the same medium was not even in the realm of imagination until that day."

On her Web page, Smith writes, "The clay is the book where I have found my own history … the story of an end of a civilization and beginning of another. … I often consider it like archeology, done with tiny knives and a shovel. Up close, I have smelled the eons of shale of millions of years and the fossils of roses clutched yet in the clay. I walked ancient and gigantic tracks and left mine in the shallow seabed of this ancient plain."

Smith's impressive murals are found throughout the United States and abroad, including panels at the Lincoln Park Zoo in Chicago. Seven of her works are listed in a catalog of significant public works by American artists, published by the Smithsonian American Art Museum. She has been featured in the Home and Garden Network television series "Master Artist" and in numerous other media.

In telling the story of humanity's quest for learning, Mara Smith included sculpted figures from early literature and images from the exploration of outer space.

Man's Search for Knowledge through the Ages

As the early morning light casts the sun's first rays on the eastern edge of Nichols Library, an enduring monument entitled *Man's Search for Knowledge through the Ages* emerges from the darkness. This beautiful bas-relief sculpture, carefully carved in brick, was created by renowned Seattle artist Mara Smith.

Using a technique that is more than 3,000 years old, Smith symbolically tells the story of the human quest for learning. On the left are open books, the solar system, life's early beginnings in the sea, and the Tree of Knowledge. These objects flow into the middle of the curved mural, bringing forth images of mathematics, mysticism, music, architecture, and literature. *Hamlet's* Ophelia and "poor Yorick" take center stage. Trumpeters and drummers, representing the parades that have passed by the library for many years, become benevolent Pied Pipers, leading everyone into the future as a space station and an astronaut take our search for knowledge into other parts of the universe. The interplay of light and shadows, as the sun moves throughout the day, creates a three-dimensional scene that is constantly changing.

This intricate brick mural is made of 1,700 bricks. To create the piece, the artist first drew a sketch. Then, after butting the wet clay bricks together on a large sheet of plastic on her workshop floor, she began to carve the scenes. Using common pottery hand tools, an ice pick, a broken saw blade, a curved knife, and other objects, she cut away pieces of clay and carved the detailed images. When the sculpting was finished, Smith disassembled the bricks, meticulously numbering each one. After the clay bricks were dried and fired at 2,000 degrees, the design was reconstructed in the studio and delivered to the library site. There, a team of brick masons, supervised by Smith and her assistant, Kris King, carefully installed the sculpture using the inscribed numbers as a guide.

Man's Search for Knowledge through the Ages was commissioned by the library in 1984 and first dedicated in 1987. The sculpture was given as a gift to the library by the John Hamer families in memory of their son and brother, Donald Dean Hamer. The bas-relief was one of three privately funded library pieces that became an official part of Century Walk in 1998.

Bronze Sculpture
Size: Life-size figures on a concrete pedestal
Girl: 5' 6" L x 18" H x 23" W
Boy: 5' 9" H x 14" D x 28" W

Location
Southwest corner of Nichols Library,
200 West Jefferson Avenue

Technique
Lost-wax casting process

Dedicated
November 19, 1988 and November 1, 1998

#9

Reading Children
By Dennis V. Smith

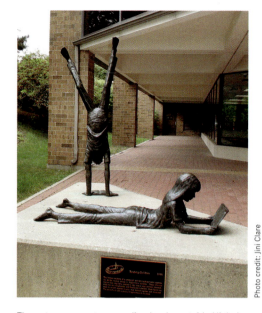

These two youngsters, reading books outside Nichols Library, have delighted children since the sculpture was first installed in 1988.

THE ARTIST

Dennis V. Smith, Sculptor, painter – One of Utah's best-known sculptors, Dennis Smith was born in 1942 and raised in the picturesque town of Alpine, Utah. He graduated from Brigham Young University and attended the Royal Academy of Art in Copenhagen. Smith's sculptures have been installed in 123 public locations in the United States and abroad. One of his works, *Signing the Constitution*, was placed in American Embassies in London and Moscow in 1989. A third casting of the piece is in the U.S. Embassy in Prague. His works have also been installed in Japan, Denmark, the Ukraine, and other foreign lands. Smith is well known as a sculptor of Latter-day Saint themes, including a monument to women and ten other sculptures in Nauvoo, Illinois. The artist frequently features children in his works, capturing their spontaneity and innocence as they explore the world around them.

Smith is an accomplished painter, skilled in oils and mixed media. He also writes poetry and is a former columnist for a daily Salt Lake City newspaper. His column and a recent book are titled *Meanderings*.

Sculptor Dennis Smith frequently features children in his works, capturing their spontaneity and innocence as they explore the world around them.

Reading Children

Two barefoot children, about 10 years old, embody the joy of reading on the patio of one of Naperville's award-winning libraries. The girl is relaxed, stretched out on the ground, fully absorbed in a captivating book. The boy is more playful, reading his book while precariously balancing his body in a handstand. Various textures of hair, clothing, and skin on the bronze figures reveal the artist's detailed modeling of the children, originally done in clay.

Created by renowned Utah artist Dennis Smith, *Reading Children* is characterized by the artist's style of figurative realism, which focuses on gestural spontaneity and exuberance for life. According to Smith, "What has been important to me is to be able to capture the vibrancy of gesture in such a way that you don't think about the form itself but how children feel." He adds, "The child takes on a metaphorical context. Children are metaphors for people in general and for that part of our spirit which is light. The sculptures show the positive spirit children have toward life that we often lose as we grow older. They become the metaphor for our greatest aspirations and our dreams."

The sculpture was presented to "the people of Naperville" in 1988 by former library trustee and board president Doris Wood, who first saw the artist's works in a sculpture garden in Nauvoo, Illinois. *Reading Children* was a gift from Doris, her late husband, Warren, and their seven children. It was one of three artworks that private individuals commissioned during the mid-1980s to enhance the new Nichols Library building. Their generosity helped to make the library a cultural, as well as an educational, center in the community. The sculptures became an official part of Century Walk in 1998, during the Naperville Public Libraries' 100th anniversary year.

Bronze Sculpture
Size: Life-size sculpture, 48" H x 30" W x 25" D, seated on a 4' plaza bench

Location
Northeast corner of Washington Street and Chicago Avenue

Technique
Lost-wax casting process

Dedicated
June 13, 1999

#10

Genevieve
By Pamela S. Carpenter

Photo credit: Don Manderscheid

THE ARTIST

Pamela S. Carpenter, Sculptor – Pamela S. Carpenter, formerly a resident of Naperville and later Glen Ellyn, was born in Kokomo, Indiana, in 1956. Self-taught in figurative realism, this artist is skilled in sculpting, mold making, wax casting, wax chasing, metal finishing, and patination. Carpenter studied at the Johnson Atelier Sculpture Foundation Studio in Mercerville, New Jersey, and refined her skills at the Palette & Chisel Academy of Fine Arts in Chicago. Before beginning her career as a sculptor, she studied fashion design and marketing at Purdue University and raised a family.

In approaching the *Genevieve* sculpture, Carpenter first spent months "getting to know" the influential writer – talking with her family and friends to learn about her personality, reading Genevieve Towsley's columns to understand the impact of her words, watching videos to capture her smile, and borrowing photos of the jewelry she wore to ensure that she would accurately portray the woman. In a *Chicago Tribune* interview, Carpenter said that she chose to portray Genevieve at 72 because Towsley was already a local legend at that age and was still healthy and active. In that same article, Carpenter explained, "Bronze sculpting is very technical in nature, with many steps involved. The creative part is re-creating someone's personality, the glint in their eyes, and offering a look into their soul."

After completing *Genevieve*, Carpenter was commissioned by the Century Walk Board to coordinate *Horse Market Days*, which is located at Naper Settlement. One of three artists involved in creating that dynamic work of art, she sculpted the young boy, again demonstrating her expertise in capturing the human form and emotions. Carpenter has also completed commissions for the City of Chicago, the Palette & Chisel Academy of Fine Arts, the Jesuit Partnership, and private collections.

Genevieve

With precise attention to detail and an emotional connection to her subject resulting from months of research, sculptor Pamela S. Carpenter re-creates the warmth and personality of a legendary Naperville author, historian, and activist in the bronze sculpture *Genevieve*.

The sculpture features Genevieve Brayton Towsley at age 72, sitting on a park bench, writing in a tablet with a treasured pen. The author is wearing a favorite sweater, adorned with a grapevine. An open space on the bench beside her invites visitors to sit with Genevieve and glance at the notes for her next story. A poem about Genevieve, written by the artist, is displayed next to the sculpture.

For over 45 years, Genevieve Towsley chronicled the history of this growing community as a columnist for the *Naperville Clarion* and later for the *Naperville Sun*. She wrote features, human interest stories, personals, and a column for the local college crowd. This kind-hearted and courageous woman often addressed controversial issues and, through the power of her pen, helped to integrate Centennial Beach, assist people in need, bring attention to the plight of migrant workers, and influence the growth of Naperville.

She is best known for her "Grapevine" column and "Sky-Lines," a carefully researched series of articles that became a fascinating archive of Naperville's past. In honor of the nation's 1976 bicentennial, the *Naperville Sun* published a collection of her historical columns in the book entitled *A View of Historic Naperville*. The out-of-print book was reprinted for the dedication of the sculpture in 1999, through the generosity of Dwight and Ruth Yackley and the *Naperville Sun*. Symbolically, the sculpture is near the entrance to a bookstore, a short distance from the original location of the *Naperville Clarion* and the *Naperville Sun*.

Pamela Carpenter carefully sculpted the life-size *Genevieve* in clay, as seen in the top photograph. When sitting on the bench next to the finished bronze figure, visitors can look down on Genevieve's writing tablet and read the notes for her next "Grapevine" column.

Clay-relief Mosaic Mural
Size: 6' H x 20' W

Location
West wall of Anderson's Bookshop,
123 West Jefferson Avenue

Technique
Carving, coloring, glazing, firing, and assembling over 400 clay tiles

Student Dedication
May 28, 1999

Century Walk Dedication
June 13, 1999

#11

River of Life

By Junior High and High School Students from Naperville Community Unit School District 203

The four clay-relief story quilts that comprise *River of Life* are side by side on the outdoor wall of Anderson's Bookshop. They are united by a river that runs through all four quilts with the words: "Naperville friends and families are like streams that flow into and energize the river of life."

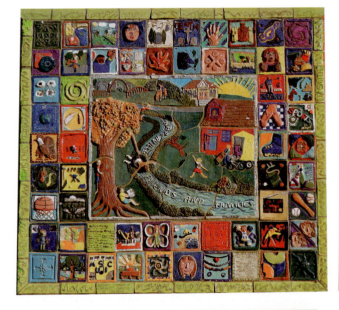

Photo credits: Don Manderscheid

The Artists – The large tile scenes in the center of each *River of Life* quilt were designed and created by ceramics class students at Naperville Central High School. The 240 smaller tiles that surround the large scenes were created by students from Jefferson, Kennedy, Lincoln, Madison, and Washington junior high schools. The students in this photo came together to dedicate the mural before their 1999 school year ended.

The tiles in the *River of Life* mural capture the memories, experiences, and hopes of Naperville's youth. Friends, family, pets, gardening, and sports are popular themes represented in the story quilts.

The River of Life

The diversity of Naperville life near the end of the twentieth century is celebrated by four clay-relief story quilts, mosaics made up of individual tiles created by more than 300 local students. Placed side by side to create the *River of Life* mural, the quilts showcase the memories, experiences, and hopes of Naperville's youth.

At the center of each intricate quilt is a large 40" x 48" panel, colorfully depicting scenes of daily life in this community. The four panels are united by a river that runs through them with the words: "Naperville friends and families are like streams that flow into and energize the river of life." Designed and created by ceramics class students at Naperville Central High School, the panels illustrate a variety of activities that were meaningful to the teens, such as a boy swinging on a tire from a tree, a girl playing ball with her dog, a teen paddle boating on the river, a child reading a book, two people washing a car, couples dancing on a stage, a young man using a laptop computer, a family picnicking together, kids playing sports, and two young women graduating from high school. A school mascot, Centennial Beach, a roller coaster, the Chicago skyline, and the Earth viewed from outer space are also shown, representing past memories and future dreams of the youth.

Sixty 8" x 8" tiles surround each of the large panels and were created by students from Jefferson, Kennedy, Lincoln, Madison, and Washington junior high schools. These 240 smaller tiles illustrate objects, people, and scenes important in the young artists' lives. Music, sports, theater, pets, peace, wildlife, jewelry, friends, faith, and cars are some of the recurring themes. Many images represent the diversity of cultures in Naperville.

Inspired by the storytelling quilts hand painted by internationally renowned artist and author Faith Ringgold, the students and their art teachers collaborated in creating this charming mural. They were guided by artist-in-residence Corinne D. Peterson, selected because of her reputation as a ceramic artist at Lillstreet Art Center in Chicago, her notable public artwork, and her skill in working with students throughout the area. The project was conceptualized and coordinated by Stacy Slack, District 203 art coordinator.

Steel and Granite Sculpture
Size: 15' H x 8' W

Location
Next to the Christian Science Reading Room,
16 East Jefferson Avenue

Technique
Steel cutouts, coated with epoxy, and granite

Dedicated
November 4, 2000

#12

Golden Rule Days

By George and Shirley Olson

"May education never become as expensive as ignorance."

Dr. Arlo L. Schilling,
North Central College president, 1960–1975

"Stay at school and don't be ashamed... that you want to learn more."

James Lawrence Nichols I,
Local business professor and textbook publisher who bequeathed $10,000 to the city of Naperville in 1895 for the establishment of a public library, from his book *The Business Guide*

"Teachers must have a loving spirit and teach each child equally regardless of heritage."

Kathryn Frey Holler,
Elementary District #78 teacher, 1931–1973

"Future developments will require that [we] re-examine... the role of public education in our society."

Dr. John F. Fields,
District 203 superintendent, 1970–1984

Photo credit: Don Manderscheid

THE ARTISTS

George C. Olson, Architect – Architect George C. Olson and artist Shirley Johnson Olson designed *Golden Rule Days* and were moved by its message of love and equality – values that were an important part of their own lives. The husband and wife team were well known in the Naperville community for their kindness to others, love of family, and business achievements. In a 2007 article about the sculpture published in the *Naperville Sun*, George Olson said, "It touched me because I'm very high on the golden rule. I think it has more international applications than we realize. In every country, in some form, they have the golden rule."

George Olson (1924–2008) was born in Brookfield, Illinois, and grew up in Riverside. He served with the Army Air Corps in Europe during World War II and later studied architecture at the Illinois Institute of Technology. While a student there, he and Shirley met on a blind date.

Shirley Johnson Olson, Fashion illustrator – Shirley Olson (1925–2004) was born in Detroit and attended Michigan State University. She was a 1946 graduate of the American Academy of Arts and a resident of the historic Three Arts Club of Chicago, a residence for young women engaged in the practice or study of the arts. She worked as a fashion illustrator, and her work was published in *Harper's Bazaar*, the *Chicago Tribune*, and other publications.

The young married couple moved to Naperville in 1951 where George eventually opened an architectural firm. Later, the Olsons purchased a grand, historic house on Jefferson Street, providing a larger home for their family as well as office space for George's growing architectural firm. The spacious Greek Revival building inspired Shirley and friends to open a yarn shop, dress shop, tearoom, and other boutiques in what became the popular Jefferson Hill Shops.

Throughout the years, George Olson earned awards and accolades for his architectural work. He was the project architect for the Yorktown Shopping Center in the 1960s, and the renovation of the Jefferson Hill Shops earned him the Merit in Architecture Award from the Northeast Illinois Chapter of the American Institute of Architects. He was active in the business community and helped Century Walk by designing foundations for several of its sculptures. George and Shirley Olson were both very involved in their church, the First Church of Christ, Scientist, in Naperville.

His talents as an architect and hers as a fashion illustrator blend beautifully in *Golden Rule Days*; George designed the schoolhouse structure, and Shirley created the human figures. Their commitment to the values of love and equality makes this sculpture a lasting legacy of their beliefs.

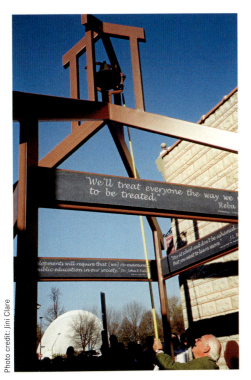

George Olson rang the school bell during the dedication of *Golden Rule Days*. The old bell, which once rang in an Indiana schoolhouse, was donated by Dr. Arlo Schilling, former president of North Central College.

Golden Rule Days

Golden Rule Days honors a local teacher whose dedication to the golden rule and innovative education touched many lives. The sculpture, designed by George and Shirley Olson of Warrenville, Illinois, is a tribute to the formative and vital role of education in this community.

Reba Otto Steck began teaching in 1914, at the age of 16, in a one-room schoolhouse on North Aurora Road. Each morning, throughout her 48-year teaching career at Crosier, Springbrook, Eola, and Wiesbrook schools, she asked her students to recite a version of the golden rule, "We'll treat everyone the way we want to be treated." Guided by this principle, when school officials refused to admit a black student, it is said that Steck told her students they could no longer begin their day by repeating the golden rule. The students talked to their parents about the injustice, years before the civil rights movement began, and school officials ultimately integrated the school.

The sculpture features silhouettes of Steck and several of her students, reading or playing near the framework of a one-room schoolhouse. Four slatelike granite slabs adorn the "walls" of the school, and quotes from local educators, etched on each of the stones, appear to be written in chalk. An old bell, which once rang in an Indiana schoolhouse, hangs from a cupola atop the structure. Donated by Dr. Arlo Schilling, former president of North Central College, the bell rings three times each day – at 8 a.m., noon, and 4 p.m. – signifying a call to education.

Three-panel Art Deco Mural
Size: 12' H x 81' W

Location
South wall of Sullivan's Steakhouse,
Chicago Avenue near Main Street

Technique
Hand painted on primed brick

Dedicated
May 27, 2001

The three panels of the art deco mural provide a dramatic glimpse into Naperville's twentieth-century history.

#13

Pillars of the Community
By Diosdado "Dodie" Mondero

Pillars of the Community, Panel 1

Photo credit: Don Manderscheid

THE ARTIST

Photo courtesy of Diosdado "Dodie" Mondero

Diosdado "Dodie" Mondero, Muralist – Abandoned as a two-week-old baby on the steps of a sanitarium in Manila, Philippines, in 1965, the future artist was quickly adopted by two elementary school teachers, Pilar and Rodolfo Mondero. Named Diosdado, meaning "God-given," the young boy was raised with love, hard work, discipline, and three older siblings. At the age of 10, he was inspired to draw after watching a portrait artist in a shopping mall. The family moved to Wheaton, Illinois, when Dodie was 13. He arrived in America with only a small bag, his clothes, and the shoes he was wearing. During his freshman year, his art teacher at Glenbard South High School soon recognized Dodie's special talents, mentored him, and later encouraged him to pursue a career in commercial art.

Mondero studied fine arts at Illinois State University and the Art Institute of Chicago and earned a degree in commercial art from the College of DuPage. For ten years, he served as art director for Artifax International Design, a Lombard-based interior design firm specializing in restaurants and other commercial businesses. His artwork and murals from that time appear in several McDonald's restaurants in the United States, Asia, and Europe. He began his own business, Mondero Studios, in 1995 and landed a big contract with Sullivan's Steakhouse creating murals for the national chain. He continues to do graphic design and artwork for private clients and major corporations, including McDonald's, Disney, and Warner Brothers. Adept in many traditional media, Mondero is also skilled with digital art forms. He is co-creator and art director of an animated cartoon series, *The Baritonios*.

Devoted to the popular culture of the 1950s, the artist owns a 1957 Chevy Bel-Air, has a diner and juke box in his home, and is inspired daily by a collection of superhero figures in his studio. Mondero's most prized possessions are the art and reference books that fill his shelves. Mondero explains, "As an artist, it's important to be informed of the past and present. Aside from art skills, knowledge is the key. It helps in the preliminary process when creating art."

Pillars of the Community

Naperville's colorful history is powerfully portrayed in this art deco mural, *Pillars of the Community*, created by Diosdado "Dodie" Mondero. The dynamic composition, bold earth-tone hues, strong shadows, and rich detail capture the attention of passersby and tempt them to discover the intriguing stories behind each vignette.

Three adjoining panels, each framed by muscular figures shouldering the ends of proscenium arches, set the stage for the history lessons. Emerging out of the steam and clouds that unify the composition are more than two dozen images, including a cast of characters, settings, and props that spotlight Naperville's heritage.

Painted on the south side of the building that occupies the original site of Naperville's historic Pre-Emption House, the mural includes:

Panel 1:

1. Peter Kroehler, who built the internationally known furniture manufacturing company that was a major employer in Naperville from the 1890s until 1978, is painted in front of the Kroehler Manufacturing Company building. Beside him is a company truck and men carrying one of the firm's upholstered sofas. Airplanes flying above the building represent the role that the factory played during World War II when it manufactured artificial limbs, ammunition boxes, airplane body parts, and propellers.

2. Ice cut from the DuPage River is delivered door-to-door in large blocks.

3. A worker from Stenger Brewery opens a barrel of hops. Young Adolph Coors worked as foreman for the Stengers from 1869 to 1872 before moving west and establishing his own brewery in Colorado.

4. Local photographers Eli Stark and Charles Koretke adjust their cameras.

5. Surveyors map out the land near a local quarry.

6. The CB&Q locomotive and Zephyr come through Naperville. The image of the Zephyr represents the streamline style of art deco.

7. A woman dives into Centennial Beach.

Panel 2:

1. The Pre-Emption House, originally located on this site, was the first hotel west of Chicago. It was an inn for traveling merchants and was the site of horse trading, depicted in Century Walk's *Horse Market Days*, and other historical events.

2. Gertrude and Frank Wehrli raised a family of 13 children in the Pre-Emption House.

3. The Civil War cannon represents Naperville's contributions to the war, as well as Civil War Days events that have taken place at Naper Settlement for many years.

4. Horses pulled heavy loads of wood for the C. B. Moore Lumber Company, which opened on Water Street in 1909. Note how the movement and composition of the horses redirect attention to the center of the mural.

5. The artist captures Naperville's original "car wash." Residents once drove their cars into the DuPage River at Eagle Street to wash their automobiles.

6. Local artist Lester Schrader preserved numerous scenes of Naperville's history with his paintings. Many of his original works of art are on permanent display at Naper Settlement.

Continued >

Photo credit: Jini Clare

Using his small drawing as a reference, artist Dodie Mondero first sketched sections of the mural on the prepared wall and then carefully painted the final images.

Pillars of the Community (Continued)

Pillars of the Community, Panel 2

Photo credit: Don Manderscheid

Photo credit: Don Manderscheid

Pillars of the Community, Panel 3

Pillars of the Community (continued)

Panel 2 (continued):

7. The Beach Inn tavern was a favorite local gathering spot along Jackson Avenue.

8. When local book publisher James Nichols I died in 1895, he left a bequest of $10,000 to purchase land and build the city's public library. The original Nichols Library still stands on Washington Street.

9. Mary ("Matie") Barbara Egermann was head librarian at Nichols Library from 1909 until 1950. During World War II, local servicemen sent her dolls from around the world. She shared her personal collection of 200 dolls with children in the community, teaching the youngsters about other countries.

10. A United States Marine brings Matie Egermann a doll for her collection while a WAVE salutes him. The two military officers honor Naperville's servicemen and servicewomen who have served the nation throughout its history.

Panel 3:

1. Leading efforts to ensure good medical care in Naperville were Grace Fredenhagen and Dr. Donald Carducci. Fredenhagen was one of the community leaders instrumental in acquiring land and cash to establish Edward Hospital.

2. Dr. Donald Carducci represents some of the first medical staff to work at Edward Hospital. The iron lung, a machine that saved the lives of many people stricken with polio, reminds us of that serious illness which so many feared in the last century.

3. The Edward Sanatorium was a highly respected center for the treatment of tuberculosis during the early- and mid-1900s. It was converted to Edward Hospital in 1955.

4. Judge Win Knoch was a key individual in acquiring land for Edward Hospital, obtaining donations from the Martin Mitchell estate, and spearheading the building of Centennial Beach.

5. Early telephone operators work at their switchboards near downtown Naperville.

6. In addition to owning the Martin quarries, George Martin II established a successful brick and tile factory in Naperville in 1871. He and his wife built the red brick Victorian mansion, Pine Craig, where they lived with their four children.

7. Caroline Martin Mitchell was the youngest surviving child of George and Sibelia Martin. Upon her death in 1937, she bequeathed her entire 204-acre estate to the community.

8. The Martin Mitchell Mansion, originally named Pine Craig, is now a museum and the focal point of Naper Settlement. It is listed on the National Register of Historic Places.

Bronze Sculptures
Sizes:
The Auction Horse – 8' H x 9' L x 2' W
The Auction Runner – 59" H x 34" W x 15" D
The Dog – 16" H x 25" L x 15" D

Location
In front of Naper Settlement's Pre-Emption House, Aurora Avenue at Webster Street

Technique
Lost-wax casting process, cast in bronze, finished with green oxide wash patina

Dedicated
June 28, 2001

#14

Horse Market Days

The Auction Horse by Robert Buono
The Auction Runner by Pamela S. Carpenter
The Dog by Torsten Muehl

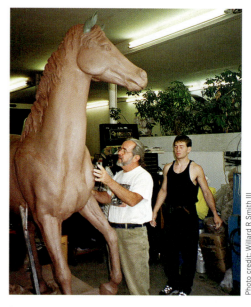

Sculptor Robert Buono discusses *The Auction Horse* clay sculpture in his studio.

Photo credit: Willard R Smith III

Photo credits: Don Manderscheid

Artists Torsten Muehl (left), Pamela Carpenter (center), and Robert Buono created this clay maquette to show the Century Walk Board their concept of *Horse Market Days*. (This photo was reprinted by permission of the *Daily Herald*, Arlington Heights, IL.)

Photo credit: *Daily Herald*, Marcelle Bright, Photographer

THE ARTISTS

Robert P. Buono, Sculptor – Born in East Chicago Harbor, Indiana, in 1947, Robert Buono was drafted by the United States Army when he was 19 and arrived in Vietnam as a combat soldier on his 20th birthday. It was an experience that he says changed his life forever. Badly wounded, the disabled veteran returned home and eventually resumed his engineering studies at Purdue University. He soon learned that his war injuries threatened his sight, and his future as an engineer was in doubt. In a fortuitous meeting on campus, a visiting Egyptian sculptor, the renowned Mustafa Naguib, told him, "Sculptors have eyes in their hands." This led to Buono's apprenticeship in sculpture and the redirection of his life. He later received a Bachelor of Fine Arts degree from Indiana University and a Master of Fine Arts degree from the School of the Art Institute in Chicago. This Vietnam veteran, who was awarded three Purple Hearts, has completed numerous works of art relating to his experience in Southeast Asia. He is the creator of the Veterans War Memorial in Lansing, Illinois, and the artist/designer for the Vietnam Veterans War Memorial in Indiana's Stoney Run County Park. In a 1989 piece entitled *Sin Loi Desidario*, he brings together forged steel, glass, neon lights, and oil on canvas to make a complex statement about separation, connections, and war. This skilled artist is talented in many media, including clay, sculpture, oils, glass, neon, pencil, wood, and others. Buono has earned numerous awards and commissions.

Pamela S. Carpenter, Sculptor – Please see Carpenter biography included with #10, *Genevieve* sculpture on page 35.

Torsten Muehl, Sculptor – Born in 1952 in Canandaigua, New York, Torsten Muehl earned a bachelor's degree in physical therapy from the University of Illinois/Chicago, a master's degree in nonprofit management from Spertus College in Chicago, and an associate's degree in art from the American Academy of Art in Chicago. He has a special interest in creating clay reliefs, especially of animals, and gets much of his inspiration at the Field Museum in Chicago. Muehl is a member of the Palette & Chisel Academy of Fine Arts in Chicago and met Carpenter and Buono through that institution. It was Muehl's interest in sculpting animals that led to his participation in the *Horse Market Days* collaboration of artists. He enjoys working in various media, including sculpture, drawing, and painting.

Horse Market Days

One of the most captivating history lessons showcased on Naperville's Century Walk is *Horse Market Days*. Set outside the Pre-Emption House, just as horse auctions were over a century ago, this sculpture depicts an event that took place the first Saturday of every month – during the spring, winter, and fall – from about 1885 until the mid-1920s. Auctioneers, farmers, and horse traders from throughout the region gathered at the Pre-Emption House to barter, bid, trade, or socialize with their neighbors. A wide variety of horses – from work, buggy, and draft horses to colts and stallions – were lined up for viewing along nearby streets. Dealers often hired young boys to help with the horses, show them to prospective buyers, and run them up Water Street hill (now Chicago Avenue), demonstrating the animals' stamina. At the end of the day, the auction runners and their dogs walked some of the horses to the railroad depot for shipment to their new owners.

Horse Market Days captures a fleeting moment at one auction as a young boy grasps the lead rope of a large horse that has just been startled by a barking dog. This snapshot in time beautifully brings to life the sudden interaction of the three figures.

Inspired by local artist Lester Schrader's oil painting, "Horse Market Day at Pre-Emption House," and coordinated by Pamela Carpenter, this sculpture is a unique collaboration of three artists – Pamela Carpenter, Robert Buono, and Torsten Muehl.

Using an old photograph of young Gus Hiltenbrand who grew up in the Pre-Emption House during that era, Carpenter authentically re-created his clothing and masterfully sculpted the auction runner. She built the basic skeletal structure from an armature of metal and foam and then sculpted the detailed figure in clay. The artist posed her own preteens to determine the auction runner's posture and expression. The boy's long-sleeve shirt, suspenders, knickers, bowler hat, knee socks, and well-worn boots clearly establish the timeframe of this historical event.

The magnificent auction horse was crafted by Robert Buono. The models for this life-size animal, shown pulling away from the boy, were a local thoroughbred and a spirited Andalusian stallion that befriended Buono at a Chicago-area stable. Buono describes the stallion as the "co-creator" of the piece. Shaped with a steel armature, the animal was lovingly sculpted out of red water-based and grey oil-based clays.

Torsten Muehl drew the initial sketch for this three-piece sculpture. With Carpenter's small terrier serving as his model, he also sculpted the animated dog. The playful pet has its ears back, its tail raised, and its hind legs ready to spring. The artist used a steel armature and oil-based clay to create the piece.

Reflecting part of local life before the automobile, *Horse Market Days* also illustrates that children and animals played a meaningful role in Naperville's history. On a symbolic level, the boy represents Naperville's unlimited energy and potential; the horse signifies the hard work and industry of Naperville, and the dog symbolizes the community's love of life and play.

Bronze Sculpture
Size: Life-size action figure,
5' 4" H x 2' 6" W x 5' 2" D on a 4' base

Location
Championship Plaza, between Cardinal Stadium and Merner Field House, on the North Central College campus

Technique
Lost-wax casting process

Dedicated
October 20, 2001

#15

College, Community and Country

By Shirley McWorter-Moss

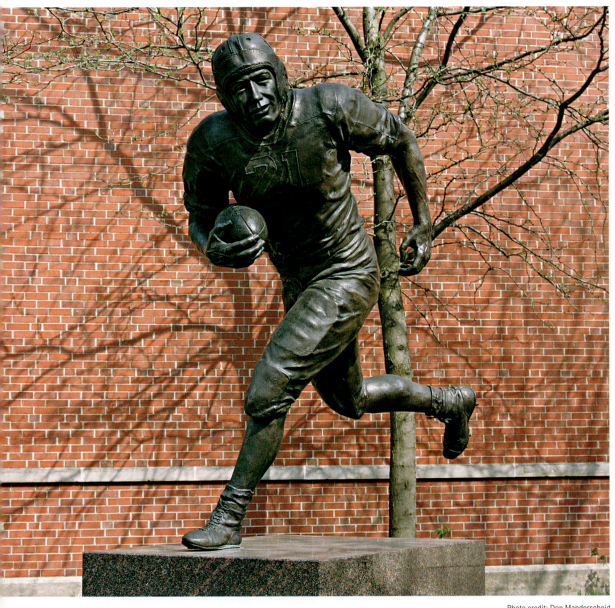

Photo credit: Don Manderscheid

THE ARTIST

Shirley McWorter-Moss, Sculptor – While the artistic talents of Shirley Moss were apparent to everyone from the time she was a young child, her latent creative vocation took a circuitous route through mathematics and aeronautical engineering before emerging as a full-time career.

Recognizing that their daughter was gifted with special abilities, Shirley Moss's parents cultivated her skills while she was in elementary school. When she was a teen, they encouraged her to enroll in a pilot program at the Cleveland Institute of Art. Four years in the program provided her with a solid foundation in art and several scholarship offers. Moss continued her art studies at Fenn College in Cleveland and at Ohio University in Athens while earning a Bachelor of Science degree in education.

A strong interest in mathematics led her to the aerospace industry in California where she initially worked as a thermal stress analyst. She later returned to the education field to teach high school math and aeronautical engineering. She received a master's degree in education from the United States International University–San Diego.

Moss eventually resumed her art studies, focusing on life sculpture and bronze casting. She began her professional art career in 1996 with a commissioned bronze sculpture that was installed in the permanent collection of the DuSable Museum of African American History in Chicago. Her life-size bust of George Allen is part of the permanent exhibit in the Pro Football Hall of Fame in Canton, Ohio.

Moss was selected to create two of the sculptures for Century Walk – *College, Community and Country* and *Veterans' Valor*. Her figurative realism style, combined with in-depth research, attention to detail, and the incorporation of personality traits of each of her subjects, brings powerful and personal elements to these works of art. She works out of her Anaheim, California, studio.

Bill Shatzer was considered by many to be the best running back in the nation when he graduated from North Central College in 1942. Following graduation, this all-around athlete enlisted in the United States Navy Air Corps. Ultimately assigned to a Navy patrol squadron in the Aleutian Islands, he was listed as "missing in action" in 1944, during World War II.

College, Community and Country

Legendary in his feats on the football field, Bill Shatzer was also heroic in his service to the nation. *College, Community and Country*, beautifully sculpted by Shirley McWorter-Moss, serves as a tribute to a great young man who excelled in all that he did and who willingly gave of himself to benefit others.

William Shatzer II was only one-and-a-half years old when his father – a hero of the deadly World War I Battle of the Argonne Forest – died. Unable to raise their family on her own, the toddler's widowed mother moved with her three young children from Pennsylvania to the Mooseheart orphanage in Illinois. There, the child grew into a young man who demonstrated great gifts in academics, sports, and leadership.

Pursuing his goal of a college education, in 1938 Shatzer enrolled in a small college just 14 miles away – North Central College. It was on this campus that he established his reputation as one of the finest athletes ever to wear the Cardinal uniform. He was considered by many to be the best running back in the nation when he graduated in 1942. This football legend was a great all-around athlete who won eleven letters while in college, excelling in football, basketball, baseball, and track.

Following his graduation from North Central College in June of 1942, Shatzer enlisted in the United States Navy Air Corps and was called to active duty two months later. Assigned to the Iowa Naval Training Station in Iowa City, he gained national fame for his brilliant record with the Seahawks, the football team of the Iowa naval preflight school. He was signed by the Detroit Lions and planned to join the professional football team after completing his military service.

This local hero received his ensign's commission in June of 1943 and married his college sweetheart, Sue Truesdell, two days later. After completing his final flight training, he was assigned to a Navy patrol squadron in the Aleutian Islands. He left for overseas duty on April 16, 1944, and a month later his family received word that he was "missing in action." His son, William Warren Shatzer III, was born two days after his family received the dreaded message.

In creating this life-size sculpture, McWorter-Moss studied old photographs of Shatzer and researched football gear of the era. She simulated the hand stitching on the helmet and accurately portrayed the young athlete with the loose-fitting socks that he typically wore. With great detail and sensitivity, she dramatically captured this athlete in motion, preserving his legacy and providing a constant reminder of a brief life well lived.

Stained-glass Window
Size: 20' H x 16' W

Location
South wall of Van Buren Avenue parking deck, between Washington and Main streets

Technique
Leaded stained glass with painted details

Dedicated
November 23, 2001

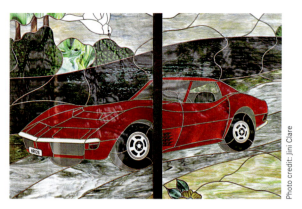

Cars of the Century is a unique tribute to the variety of auto dealerships that sold and serviced cars locally during the twentieth century.

#16
Cars of the Century
By The Artists of Sheri Law Art Glass, Ltd.

Photo credit: Jini Clare

THE ARTISTS

Artists of Sheri Law Art Glass, Ltd. – *Cars of the Century* was designed and created by a team of seven artists at Sheri Law Art Glass, Ltd. Together, they determined the theme, designed the window, selected the stained glass, cut the individual pieces, leaded each piece of glass, and assembled the unusual work of art. Some of the pieces were "sand carved," and details were hand painted on several individual images.

Sheri Law Art Glass, located in Homer Glen, Illinois, provides imaginative custom art glass for both residential and commercial clients. The firm employs the adept talents of its artisans through drawing, glass cutting, carving and etching glass, painting, and gilding.

Four classic automobile models are featured on this stained-glass window, including a 1909 Model T touring car, a 1930 Model A Ford, a 1972 Oldsmobile Vista Cruiser, and a 1968 Chevrolet Corvette Stingray, seen on the previous page. Artistic license added rich hues to several vehicles.

Cars of the Century

The story of the automobile was an important tale during the twentieth century, and the impact of cars and dealerships in this community reflected many of the national trends. As Naperville grew from a small town to a thriving suburban city, commuters and car pools became a familiar part of daily life. The make and model of a favorite car were forever stamped in personal memories and helped define each decade.

This colorful stained-glass window, *Cars of the Century*, is a unique tribute to the variety of auto dealerships that sold and serviced cars locally. Longtime residents are familiar with the names of the dealerships that were located downtown until the mid-1960s. Cromer Motor Company, situated at the northeast corner of Chicago Avenue and Main Street, was the original Ford distributorship in northeastern Illinois. During the early 1900s, vehicles were transported from Chicago by horse and wagon to Cromer's garage where final assembly took place. The Netzley family operated the Netzley Chrysler-Plymouth franchise for over 50 years at the corner of Chicago Avenue and Washington Street. The other dealerships were the Huffstettler family's Huff Chevrolet, Charley Burgess's Kaiser-Frazer, Brummel Motor Company's Buick dealership, Mueller Pontiac, Colonial Motor Sales (Buick-Pontiac), and Koller Dodge. Many of these businesses later moved to Ogden Avenue, changed owners, or ceased to exist. Whatever their fate, the auto businesses played a key role in the development of the community, supporting its fund-raisers, sponsoring its sports teams, and adding to the vitality of the area.

To highlight Naperville's love affair with the automobile, the artists selected four classic models to travel along the winding road of time. Although it is rumored that Henry Ford once said, "You can paint it any color, so long as it's black," artistic license added rich hues to several vehicles, giving this vibrant window the drama that captures the attention of passersby throughout the day and night. Artists used 26 different types of glass with varied textures, colors, and density. This striking, insulated window is made up of 1,114 separate pieces of glass in 16 panels.

The history lesson begins with a 1909 Model T touring car, traveling along a country lane with its convertible top down. Just ahead is a deep blue 1930 Model A Ford, blended with characteristics of the later Model B. To reflect the growth of Naperville's families and popular station wagons of the era, a canary yellow 1972 Oldsmobile Vista Cruiser takes its place in this parade of cars. In the lead, a bright red 1968 Chevrolet Corvette Stingray speeds into the next century, leaving cherished memories behind.

Bronze Sculpture
Size: Life-size children 42" H x 29" W x 21" D on a 6' bench

Location
The west side of Main Street between Chicago and Jackson avenues

Technique
Lost-wax casting process

Dedicated
November 5, 2002

Two young children, dressed in period costumes, posed as models for this sculpture.

#17

A Lifetime Together
By Emanuel Martinez

Photo credit: Don Manderscheid

50

THE ARTIST

Emanuel Martinez, Sculptor, painter, muralist – Emanuel Martinez is an award-winning artist of national significance – a sculptor, painter, and muralist who has mastered numerous media including bronze, stone, terra cotta, charcoal, oil, and acrylic. An influential contributor to the Chicano Movement, which began during the turbulent 1960s, Martinez has created many works in pursuit of social justice. In 1967, the Roman Catholic bishop of Los Angeles commissioned him to create *Farm Workers' Altar,* which was later used during an important civil rights Mass. The altar is one of this artist's three works that are part of the permanent collection of the Smithsonian American Art Museum in Washington, D.C.

Born in 1947 in Denver, Colorado, Martinez overcame a childhood of poverty and troubles through his art. When the nurse at a boys' school witnessed the masterpieces that the incarcerated youth created with burnt match heads on paper towels, a new and positive vision emerged for the talented 13-year-old boy. He began to see himself as an artist, and teachers encouraged his efforts. As an adult, Martinez was strongly influenced by David Alfaro Siqueiros and was invited to study with the famous artist in Mexico. Today, Martinez works in his art studio overlooking Red Rocks Park in Morrison, Colorado.

Emanuel Martinez and his wife, Maria, sit next to the bronze children and share *A Lifetime Together*.

A Lifetime Together

The innocence of childhood in this small Midwestern town during the late 1920s is beautifully portrayed in *A Lifetime Together* by renowned artist Emanuel Martinez.

The bronze sculpture depicts the love story of Jane Latshaw and William "Billy" Scherer. These charmingly crafted children sit on a park bench, holding hands, smiling at one another while Jane's schoolbooks rest on Billy's lap. They seem unaware of visitors who may join them on the bench. On display beside them are two special memories – a copy of a letter that Jane wrote to an ailing Billy while in elementary school and a note that Billy signed with a college friend, betting 50 cents that he would someday marry his childhood sweetheart.

The youngsters were born in Naperville in 1918, fell in love as third-grade students at Ellsworth Elementary School, attended high school together at Naperville High School, and began their 60-year marriage in 1941. Descendants from historic families in this community, Jane is the great-granddaughter of John Naper, brother of Naperville's founder, Joseph Naper. Billy was the grandson of Christian Scherer, who opened Scherer Hardware at the southeast corner of Jefferson Avenue and Washington Street in the 1880s. Billy's father, William Christian Scherer, continued to operate the hardware store until 1946.

A Lifetime Together is one of two sculptures commissioned for Century Walk by the couple's children – John, James, and Susan. John Scherer, CEO and founder of the nationally known Video Professor software training company, donated $100,000 toward the sculptures. He also endowed two scholarships in his parents' names. The gifts, given a few months after his father's death in April of 2002, were inspired by photographs in a family scrapbook and by his mother, an educator. "My mother would always tell me, 'Never forget where you came from,'" John Scherer explained.

This delightful sculpture shares the charming love story of Jane Latshaw and William "Billy" Scherer, two children who grew up in Naperville and began their 61-year marriage in 1941. Descendants from historic families in the community, they represent the innocence of childhood in this small Midwestern town during the late 1920s.

Bronze Sculpture
Size: 5' 10" H x 3' 3" W x 3' D

Location
Near the Athletic Plaza at the south entrance of Naperville Central High School, 440 West Aurora Avenue

Technique
Lost-wax casting process

Dedicated
November 6, 2002

#18

Be the Best That You Can Be
By Emanuel Martinez

Emanuel Martinez took these photos of the clay sculpture in his Colorado art studio.

Photo credits: Emanuel Martinez

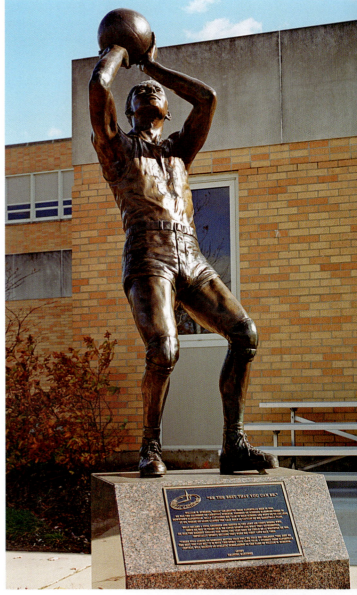

Photo credit: Don Manderscheid

52

THE ARTIST
Emanuel Martinez, Sculptor, painter, muralist –
Please see Martinez' biography included with #17, *A Lifetime Together*.

Emanuel Martinez captures the intensity of Billy Scherer's concentration as he attempts a free throw for his 1936 basketball team at Naperville High School. As an adult, Scherer always taught his children, "Be the best that you can be." It is his ethics of hard work and determination that are memorialized in this sculpture.

Be the Best That You Can Be

In *Be the Best That You Can Be*, nationally renowned sculptor Emanuel Martinez captures the 1936 Naperville High School basketball team captain, William H. "Billy" Scherer, as he attempts a free throw. The grandson of Christian Scherer, founder of Scherer Hardware Store in downtown Naperville, Billy Scherer always taught his children, "Be the best that you can be." He also cautioned them that, in life, there will always be someone who is better.

It is Billy Scherer's ethics of hard work and determination that are memorialized in this sculpture and in two scholarships established by John Scherer, one of his sons and CEO/founder of Video Professor. Endowed by a $500,000 gift to the Naperville Education Foundation, the scholarships are awarded each year to two graduating seniors at Naperville Central High School. One scholarship, in honor of his father, is earmarked for a male or female student voted "best athlete of the year." The second scholarship is awarded to a student who plans to pursue a career in education, in honor of his mother, Jane Latshaw Scherer. A former kindergarten teacher and Billy's childhood sweetheart, she also graduated from Naperville High School in 1936.

Copper Sculpture
Size: 6½' H x 25½" W x 26" D
on an 8' H base

Location
Burlington Square Park, just south of the Naperville train station

Technique
Pressed copper sheet metal, mechanically joined and soldered

Dedicated
Decoration Day, May 31, 1926

Rededicated
Memorial Day Weekend, May 25, 2003

#19

Spirit of the American Doughboy
By E. M. Viquesney
Restored by Giorgio Gikas of Venus Bronze Works, Inc.

Dee Pasternak (left) and Sergeant of the Guard Jack Shiffler stand near the *Spirit of the American Doughboy* sculpture at the rededication ceremony in 2003. Pasternak played a major role in forming the Save Our Doughboy committee and restoring the 1926 sculpture.

Photo credit: *Naperville Sun*, Leslie Barbaro, Photographer

Photo credits: Don Manderscheid

THE ARTIST

E. M. Viquesney, Sculptor – Ernest Moore Viquesney (1876–1946) was born in Spencer, Indiana, and learned the trade of stone carving, sculpting, and engraving from his father who owned a monument business there. After serving in the Spanish-American War, Viquesney married and eventually moved to Americus, Georgia, where he designed statuary for Confederate soldier memorials erected at the Andersonville Prison Cemetery and Park. He also worked for several monument companies over the years. It was in Americus that he created *Spirit of the American Doughboy*. Copyrighted by the artist in 1920, the sculpture was named the official World War I National Memorial by The American Legion. In 1922, Viquesney returned to Spencer where he continued his art work and other business ventures.

Spirit of the American Doughboy

Inspired by tales of returning soldiers and John McCrae's World War I poem, "In Flanders Fields," sculptor E. M. Viquesney was determined to honor the bravery and sacrifices of the American men who fought for democracy in Europe during "the War to End All Wars." The soldiers, affectionately known as "doughboys," faced brutal conditions on the battlefields, and many never came home.

At least 135 copies of his sculpture, *Spirit of the American Doughboy*, were dedicated in communities around the country to honor fallen sons and veterans. In Naperville, the names of seven local doughboys who died while serving their country are engraved on a nearby plaque.

Through intensive research, the use of uniformed doughboys as models, and the study of photographs, the artist captured minute details of the soldier in battle. Viquesney once wrote, "Look into those eyes which you will note are gazing straight ahead – eyes full of confidence, bravery, power, and yet eyes that carry a dew of suffering, pain, and agony." The sculptor portrayed the doughboy wearing a flat steel helmet. The soldier's right arm is reaching upward, preparing to throw a hand grenade. In this left hand, he is carrying a bayoneted rifle. A bedroll is draped across his back, and a gas mask pouch falls across his chest. A cartridge belt is fastened around his waist, and the doughboy's bloused trousers are wrapped tightly below the knee. The brave young man is walking across the barren ground of "No Man's Land" in hob-nailed shoes, with two burned-out tree stumps and barbed wire at his feet.

According to Earl D. Goldsmith, who wrote about the history of this mass-produced sculpture, most of the doughboys created by Viquesney were made of pressed copper or bronze alloy sheets. Each doughboy was made up of more than 75 die-stamped pieces, which were then welded together over an internal metal frame. This doughboy sculpture was probably fabricated by the Friedley-Voshardt Company in Chicago.

Originally dedicated in 1926, a gift from American Legion Post 43, Naperville's statue gradually fell into disrepair. By 2001, the doughboy was missing his right hand and rifle, and sections of stump and barbed wire were gone. A concerned local artist and Century Walk Board member, Dee Pasternak, brought the doughboy's condition to the attention of the Naperville Park District, the Century Walk Board, the VFW, and The American Legion and asked them to investigate how the memorial could be restored. Within a few months, the Save Our Doughboy committee was formed, a community-wide fund-raising campaign was begun, and a sculptural restoration firm, Venus Bronze Works, was identified in Detroit. With a major grant from Century Walk and donations from other groups and individuals, over $100,000 was raised to restore the sculpture and enhance the plaza surrounding it.

On Memorial Day weekend in 2003, a grateful community welcomed the doughboy home. More than 500 Naperville residents gathered in Burlington Square to rededicate this historic sculpture and fulfill the artist's wish – " I hope that he may be a constant inspiration and call to all, teaching us what real Americanism is, what it does, and how it safeguards our homes and our country."

Before restoration began on this World War I sculpture, the doughboy was missing his right hand and rifle, and sections of tree stump and barbed wire were gone (top photo). The sculpture was painstakingly restored by Giorgio Gikas of Venus Bronze Works, Inc.

Bronze Sculpture
Size: 13" W x 4¼" H x 3¼" D

Location
30 West Jefferson Avenue

Technique
Lost-wax casting process

Dedicated
June 20, 2003

#20

Yes We Can!

By Earl Swanson

The small plaza, granite benches, and pedestal were designed by architect George Olson and became part of Century Walk's twentieth piece, *Yes We Can!*

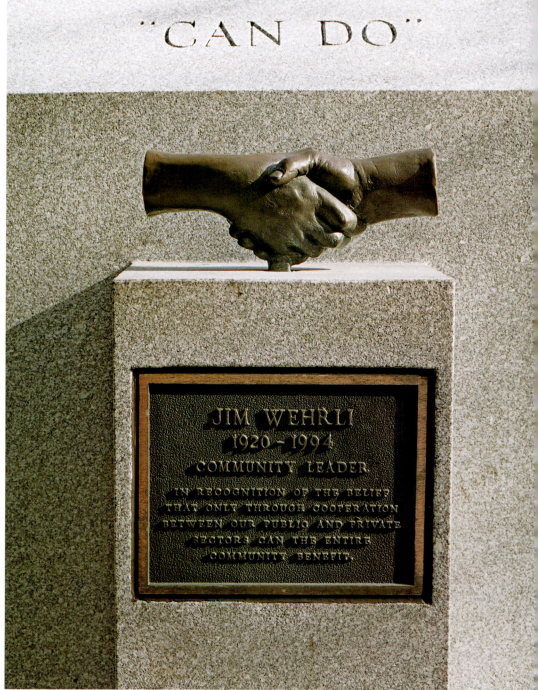

Photo credit: Don Manderscheid

THE ARTIST

Earl E. Swanson, Jr., Sculptor – Earl "Bud" Swanson (1927–2006) was a man of many talents. The founder of the nonprofit Danada Sculpture Gardens Association, he was also an accomplished artist, 18-year York Township Highway Commissioner, Republican Committeeman for DuPage County, musician and composer, scratch golfer, and family man.

Born in 1927 in Oak Park, Illinois, Swanson spent his childhood in Villa Park and dropped out of high school to join the Navy in 1945. When he returned from the South Pacific, he finished high school and earned a bachelor's degree from Elmhurst College. His love for the arts started at an early age and continued throughout his life. He played for the DuPage Symphony Orchestra as a young man and began to study sculpture years later, after he retired from the highway department. Swanson studied with noted Egyptian sculptor Mustafa Naguib at the Mustafa Naguib School of Sculpture in Chicago and became associated with the school as an instructor. He also attended the Scottsdale Artists' School in Arizona.

In 1990, Swanson founded the Danada Sculpture Gardens Association, a nonprofit organization created "to recognize and promote sculpture for the cultural and economic benefit of the entire community, to develop community support systems for the arts, and to foster art appreciation by providing a botanical showcase for sculptural art in DuPage County." Working with a dedicated group of volunteers, donors, and corporations, the association presented nine fine sculpture shows from 1992 to 2000. Several Century Walk artists displayed their sculptures in these shows at Cantigny Park.

Many of Swanson's pencil portraits and bronze sculptures are in public and private collections around the country. Five of his life-size sculptures, all of which feature children, can be seen in Lombard. They are *Hometown Pledge, Some Day Soon, A Penny a Day, An Apple a Day,* and *Your Turn*. His sculptures and those of other artists helped Lombard achieve statewide recognition for its public art program.

Yes We Can!

A simple handshake – in earlier days a handshake was much more than a business formality. It was an agreement, an unwritten contract, an honored promise. This handshake, created in bronze, represents the long-standing partnership that exists between the private and public sectors in Naperville. *Yes We Can!* recalls the specific efforts of local merchants and government officials who worked together to restore and rejuvenate a threatened downtown in the early 1970s.

The sculpture and its surrounding plaza tell the story of Naperville's "Can-Do" spirit. At a time when this small town's economic future was challenged by regional shopping malls, a group of concerned business leaders formed a partnership with city government and met those challenges strategically. Under the leadership of Harold Kester, Bill Luxion, John Prescott, Bob Wallace, Jim Wehrli, and Warren Wood, they formed CANDO, the Central Area Naperville Development Organization, in 1972.

For 29 years, this nonprofit organization spearheaded innovations and improvements that led to the vitality of the central business district today. Through the efforts of CANDO, a plan was developed for the downtown area, the DuPage River was identified as a potential riverfront park, parking became free, a parking deck was built, streetscapes were enhanced, trees and flowers were planted, holiday lights were hung, and the downtown was improved and energized. As a result, Naperville's central business district remains a model for other communities that want their downtown areas to become centers of commerce and activity.

Created by Earl Swanson in 1995, the sculpture was commissioned by CANDO to honor the late Jim Wehrli and was installed in front of Wehrli's appliance store. When CANDO disbanded in 2001, the artwork was donated to Century Walk. Century Walk asked architect George Olson to design the small plaza, granite benches, and pedestal and later dedicated *Yes We Can!* as its twentieth piece.

In 1995, CANDO commissioned Earl Swanson (top photo) to create a bronze sculpture in honor of the late Jim Wehrli. The artwork was donated to Century Walk when CANDO disbanded in 2001. Century Walk added other features to enhance the sculpture and dedicated *Yes We Can!* in 2003. (The top photo was reprinted by permission of the *Daily Herald*, Arlington Heights, IL.)

World Trade Center Steel Beam, Granite, and Limestone Sculpture
Size: 9' 6" H x 7' 9" W x 7' 9" D

Location
Along the Riverwalk, between the Naperville Municipal Center and the DuPage River

Technique
Hand carving, chiseling, diamond-point etching

Dedicated
September 11, 2003

World Trade Center survivor Joseph Dittmar spoke about the events of September 11, 2001, and the meaning of freedom during the dedication of the Commander Dan Shanower/ September 11 Memorial in 2003. Hundreds of area residents attended the ceremonies.

#21

Lean on US
By Bill Cooper

Photo credit: Don Manderscheid

THE ARTIST

Bill C. Cooper, Sculptor – Born in 1948 in Oak Park, Illinois, Bill Cooper is a sculptor and professional memorialist with over 30 years' experience working with granite. He was an art major at MacMurray College in Jacksonville, Illinois, and also studied at the Toledo Museum of Art in Ohio. Bill and his wife, Genie, own St. Joe Monument Works in Benton Harbor, Michigan. Although their firm specializes in the design and engraving of personal cemetery monuments, the couple has also created a number of civic memorials in southwestern Michigan.

In a personal story related to the Coopers' emotional creation of *Lean on US*, Bill and Genie had enjoyed lunch with friends at the World Trade Center a week before the September 11th attacks. They then left for a vacation in Italy. As they were returning to the United States the following week, their flight was diverted to Nova Scotia when the events of 9/11 prompted the FAA to ground thousands of flights across the continent. The artist and his wife felt honored to even touch the beam that became the centerpiece of this sculpture.

A large gash in the granite base of this sculpture represents the crash of American Airlines Flight 77 (top photo). Commander Dan Shanower's footprint is engraved on the granite pentagon, and the emblems of the New York City Police and Fire Departments and the Port Authority of New York and New Jersey are engraved on the granite pillar.

Lean on US

Along the banks of the DuPage River, in the heart of Naperville, stands a poignant memorial to a local hero and to all the innocent victims who died on September 11, 2001. At the center of the memorial is a powerful sculpture, which honors the heroes of that day and pays tribute to a nation that stands for freedom throughout the world.

Full of symbolism, the sculpture, *Lean on US*, features a 7-foot, 2,000-pound steel beam from the World Trade Center, pieces of limestone from the Pentagon, and American black granite from Pennsylvania.

The artist, Bill Cooper, positioned the steel beam and a large granite pillar on top of a large, five-sided granite base. The pillar is engraved with the emblems of the New York City Police and Fire Departments and the Port Authority of New York and New Jersey. Also engraved is the number 93, subtly paying tribute to the heroes of United Airlines Flight 93, which crashed near Shanksville, Pennsylvania.

To symbolize the violent destruction of the World Trade Center, the beam and pillar rest precariously, at acute angles, on the granite pentagon. The beam is leaning on the solid pillar. The polished granite base is scarred by a large gash, which represents the crash of American Airlines Flight 77 into the Pentagon. The footprint of Commander Dan Shanower, a Navy intelligence officer and Naperville native who died in the Pentagon that morning, is engraved on the shiny black granite. According to Cooper, who felt honored to create this sculpture, "The main impact of this memorial comes from the World Trade Center beam, supported in its collapse by the solid assurance that we will never forget September 11."

The Commander Dan Shanower/September 11 Memorial provides a reverent setting for *Lean on US*. The result of the efforts of numerous volunteers, businesses, and residents who selflessly led and contributed to this project, the memorial contains several additional elements. *The Wall of Faces* is a 48-foot-long, precast concrete backdrop featuring the visages of 130 men, women, and children. Drawn by local schoolchildren and made into three-dimensional clay portraits by several local artists, including Dottie Farrell, Connie Simons, and Sheila Bruns, the faces celebrate the lives of September 11's innocent victims. Attached to the wall is an eternal flame. Nearby, a flagpole donated by local veterans groups proudly displays the American flag. A lone granite bench is carved with the words *Freedom Isn't Free* – the title and final words of an article that Shanower published to honor four of his shipmates who died in 1987 while serving aboard the aircraft carrier USS *Midway*. Shanower's prophetic essay concluded, "They knew the risks they were taking and gave their lives for something bigger than themselves. I'll never forget them, and I'll never forget the day I learned that freedom isn't free."

Bronze Sculpture
Size: Life-size plus one-third,
8' H x 9' W x 3' 9" D

Location
Framed by the archway of Main Street Promenade at 55 South Main Street

Technique
Lost-wax casting process

Dedicated
November 2, 2003

Representing the humble beginnings of recycling, a young boy collects cans and bottles, pulling his heavy wagon uphill.

#22
Symbiotic Sojourn
By Jeff Adams

Photo credit: Don Manderscheid

THE ARTIST

Jeff Adams, Sculptor – Jeff Adams grew up in Oregon, Illinois, a small town along the Rock River, 90 miles west of Chicago. As a teenager, he worked at a local fine-art foundry where he learned many of the techniques of sculpting and casting. In 1982, Adams graduated with a degree in civil engineering from Northern Arizona University in Flagstaff, but due to a recession, he was unable to find an engineering job at that time. In a twist of fate, the young man soon found work at a foundry in Sedona. Although it was initially a temporary career choice, the foundry work afforded Adams the opportunity to refine his skills, establish a reputation for fine patinas, and create his own sculptures.

As he gained national recognition for his work, Adams moved to Mt. Morris, Illinois, near his hometown, and ultimately opened InBronze Foundry, a full-service art casting facility that includes a studio, gallery, and foundry. By owning the foundry, he is able to control all aspects of the creative process, from concept to installation. It is this marriage of artistic intuition, design elements, theme, and craftsmanship that makes his sculptures unique.

Adams explains, "My artistic vision is to create sculptures with emotional messages that transcend the subject matter of the piece. Through my figures, I depict the invisible forces of wind and waves, the mythical process of metamorphosis, and elusive emotions exposed in a moment. As I breathe life into my sculptures, I strive to capture their spirit in the permanent solidity of bronze."

Century Walk first learned of Jeff Adams when he cast its *Genevieve* sculpture and later its three-piece *Horse Market Days* sculpture. On a visit to InBronze Foundry, board members became aware of the exceptional talent of this award-winning artist. The board commissioned him to create two pieces for Century Walk: *Symbiotic Sojourn* and *Two in a Million*.

Jeff Adams is known for numerous public and private commissions, including *Paths of Conviction, Footsteps of Fate*, a 13½-foot-high bronze sculpture of Abraham Lincoln and Sauk warrior Black Hawk, considered to be one of the finest Lincoln sculptures in the state of Illinois.

Symbiotic Sojourn

In a moving tribute to Naperville's early and significant role in recycling, sculptor Jeff Adams symbolically captures the interdependent relationship between people and the Earth in *Symbiotic Sojourn*.

This bronze sculpture features the Spirit of the Earth extending her arms over a concave, broken globe and two young children. Water flows from her hand into the pool below. The boy represents the humble beginnings of recycling – collecting cans and bottles, pulling his heavy wagon uphill. The girl – holding onto the fractured globe and gazing at our hemisphere – illustrates the caring relationship we must have with the Earth. The tree trunk – an aggregate of stacked newspapers and pop cans, recognizable at the base and then bent, crushed, and transformed into lush vegetation in the higher portions of the tree – suggests that trash can be turned into something of value.

The sculpture was inspired by the visionary activism of Barbara Ashley Sielaff, who prompted Naperville to become a national leader in recycling with the establishment of the Naperville Area Recycling Center in 1973. The environmentalist also wrote a column for the *Naperville Sun* entitled "You Can Save Our Earth," which promoted the importance of recycling. When real estate developers Dwight and Ruth Yackley first saw Adams' clay maquette of the sculpture, they asked if it could be modified to become a fountain. The couple found a place of honor for the finished piece in the courtyard of their downtown development, the Main Street Promenade. The Yackleys, owners of BBM, Inc., also made a substantial contribution to Century Walk for the creation of the sculpture.

The Spirit of the Earth (top photo) extends her arms over a broken globe and two children. In the lower photo, a small girl gazes at our hemisphere.

Bronze Sculpture
Size: Life-size figures,
6' 10" H x 3' 4" W x 3' 6" D

Location
Rotary Plaza at Fredenhagen Park along the Riverwalk

Technique
Lost-wax casting process

Dedicated
June 15, 2005

#23

Two in a Million
By Jeff Adams

Walter and Grace Fredenhagen gaze out over Fredenhagen Park, the place that once was home to their Naperville Creamery Company and later to Prince Castles Ice Cream shop.

Photo credit: Don Manderscheid

THE ARTIST
Jeff Adams, Sculptor –
Please see Adams' biography included with #22, *Symbiotic Sojourn*.

Two in a Million

They were two in a million – Walter Fredenhagen, the visionary businessman, and Grace Fredenhagen, his wife and life partner, herself a visionary in the community. Sculptor Jeff Adams beautifully captures their essence in this life-size bronze sculpture.

Placed on the site of the family's once-thriving dairy business, Walter is symbolically leaning forward with his arm outstretched, communicating that his ideas for the future are flowing through his hand into the community. Grace is at her husband's side, supportive yet contemplating visions of her own. Together they are looking at Fredenhagen Park, the place that once was home to their Naperville Creamery Company and later to Prince Castles Ice Cream shop, famed for its "One in a Million" milkshakes and cones made with square scoops of ice cream.

With the help of his wife, Walter built a business empire at this site, beginning in the 1920s with the purchase of the first plot of land. Initially, the entrepreneurs cut ice from the river, stored it in a building here, and delivered ice blocks door-to-door during the summer. Later, the couple started a dairy, producing milk, butter, and ice cream. Locals recall Walter driving the horse cart and Grace running bottles of milk to people's front doors. But Walter's visionary nature is best illustrated by his belief, at the height of the Great Depression, that people would spend a nickel on entertainment for their families. He opened the first Prince Castles Ice Cream shop here in 1931 and ultimately built 25 stores in the Chicago area. (Many were later renamed Cock Robin.) Prince Castles, a popular gathering spot for families, was once the second-largest employer in Naperville. Ray Kroc, the founder of McDonald's, sold multi-mixers for Prince Castles and fashioned his first restaurant after the local store.

Grace's vision was directed more toward the community. She was involved with many projects regarding Naperville's growth. Her inspiration and effort were instrumental in restoring and furnishing the Martin Mitchell Mansion, which later became part of Naper Settlement. Grace also played a significant role in acquiring the land that is now the Edward Hospital campus. A professional pianist with the Marshall Field Choral Society in Chicago, this talented woman helped support the family in the early years through her work in Chicago and by giving piano lessons to children.

The sculpture was financed, in part, through a donation by the Rotary Club of Naperville. Walter Fredenhagen was a founding member of the club in 1941 and was its second president. The sculpture, completed in only three-and-a-half months by Jeff Adams, was installed days before Rotary International's 100th anniversary celebration in Chicago in June of 2005.

In the top photo, the bronze figures of Walter and Grace Fredenhagen are lowered into place and installed. The bronze sculpture was originally crafted in clay in the artist's studio, as shown in the lower photo.

Mural
Size: 18' H x 70' W

Location
Alleyway between 113 and 121 South Washington Street

Technique
Trompe l'oeil scenes, hand painted with oil-based sign enamel on primed brick walls

Dedicated
October 27, 2005

This nostalgic mural engages viewers in the everyday life of a simpler, smaller Naperville of the 1960s when the town's population was less than 22,000.

#24

The Way We Were
By Marianne Lisson Kuhn and Liza Netzley-Hopkins

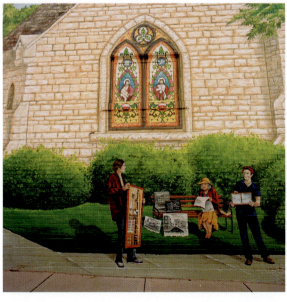
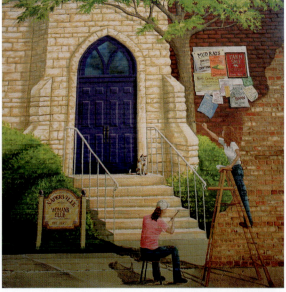

Photo credits: Don Manderscheid

THE ARTISTS

Liza Netzley-Hopkins (left) and Marianne Lisson Kuhn

Marianne Lisson Kuhn, Muralist – A fifth-generation Napervillian, Marianne Lisson Kuhn is well-known throughout the region for her detailed pen-and-ink drawings and limited-edition prints. She has depicted numerous Naperville, Sandwich Fair, and rural farm and tractor scenes, helping to preserve the area's history. Also skilled in watercolor, oil, and pastel, Kuhn possesses a style that is realistic and full of detail. Her artwork frequently features trees and vegetation. The artist was born in Aurora, Illinois, in 1955, and raised on a farm on Lisson Road. She earned a degree in fashion design and illustration from the College of DuPage.

Liza Netzley-Hopkins, Muralist – Born in 1951 in Aurora, Illinois, Liza Netzley-Hopkins is also a fifth-generation Napervillian. She grew up in a home overlooking a downtown quarry, currently the Visitor Center for the Millennium Carillon. Pursuing her interest in art, which she developed as a young child, Netzley-Hopkins studied at the Art Institute of Chicago and the College of DuPage. Professionally, she became one of the top sign painters in the Chicago area and earned numerous state and national awards for her work. Marianne and Liza frequently work together, painting murals and furniture that adorn clients' homes and businesses.

Paintings for an upcoming art show are displayed on a bench outside the Naperville Woman's Club (top photo), while a self-portrait of one of the muralists finishing the final scene of *The Way We Were* adds a personal touch to this work of art.

The Way We Were

Gone but not forgotten, several of Naperville's favorite downtown businesses and everyday scenes are captured in this nostalgic mural, *The Way We Were*. Created by local artists Marianne Lisson Kuhn and Liza Netzley-Hopkins, the detailed *trompe l'oeil* images engage viewers in the everyday life of a simpler, smaller Naperville of the 1960s when the town's population was less than 22,000. The scenes also bring back memories of fads and fashions of a colorful time in America's history. The artwork was designed by Kuhn and painted by both artists working together.

The mural begins on the left with Soukups Hardware, fondly remembered by residents for its crowded shelves and a tiny basement lined with toys. This popular store is the backdrop for a local artist as he paints a street scene of the downtown. Next door, a man in a business suit walks out of Trudy's Flowers and Gift Shop, carrying a bouquet of fresh flowers home to his wife. Teenagers gather outside of Naper Theater, a favorite hangout, while a parent in a blue Ford Mustang waits nearby. The theater marquee advertises the 2 p.m. matinee of *The Way We Were*, and posters promote *Mary Poppins* and *Butch Cassidy and the Sundance Kid*, popular movies of the era. Meanwhile, a paperboy, chased by his dog, Eddy, rides his Schwinn Sting-Ray on the sidewalk past City Hall. Mayor William Zaininger can be seen through the City Hall window, while Carl Broeker's department store is reflected in the glass. A mother in capri pants and her young daughter clutching a Mrs. Beasley doll pass by after a shopping trip to Dean's. The small boy with his Davy Crockett coonskin cap, Batman lunch pail, and fishing rod hurries along the sidewalk, possibly on his way to a nearby quarry.

Adding more personal touches to the mural, the artists place Liza's father, Clyde Netzley, on the steps of City Hall. The owner of the Netzley Chrysler-Plymouth dealership downtown, he is reading an issue of the *Clarion*. Its montage of headlines highlights some of the decade's most significant events: "President Kennedy Establishes the Peace Corps," "Dr. Martin Luther King, Jr. – I Have a Dream," "More Casualties in Vietnam," and "Man on the Moon."

The Naperville Woman's Club, housed in a former church building, is the backdrop for other cleverly placed scenes of Naperville's past. Dorcas Pearcy, owner of Toenniges Jewelers, and Shirley Baumann, a Woman's Club member and local art show volunteer, review a student's paintings that illustrate more of the town's buildings, including Prince Castles Ice Cream and Scott's dime store.

In the final scene on the right, the artists portray themselves painting the mural. A family pet named Mia sits on the steps of the church building, and notices about a Lisson Farm sale, the Mud Rats Swim Team practice at Centennial Beach, a Battle of the Bands event at the Barn, and the Saints Peter and Paul's Corn Fest are posted on the bulletin board. The unpainted edge of brick on the lower right reminds passersby that the once-unattractive brick alley wall is now a charming piece of public art for all to enjoy.

Bronze Sculpture
Size: Life-size, 6' H x 4' 3" W x 3' 3" D

Location
On the Riverwalk, just east of the Dandelion Fountain

Technique
Lost-wax casting process

Dedicated
May 1, 2006

Cast in bronze, businessman Jim Moser and Mayor Chet Rybicki survey the beautiful Riverwalk that they helped create.

#25

Riverwalk Visionaries

By Kathleen Farrell
Assisted by Dante DiBartolo,
David Standifer,
and Roberta Faulhaber

Photo credit: Friends of Community Public Art

THE ARTIST
Kathleen Farrell, Sculptor, painter, and mosaic artist –
Please see Farrell's biography with #4, *Heartland Harvest*.

Thanks to the vision of a few residents and the efforts of an entire community, a once-neglected riverfront was transformed into Naperville's crown jewel, the Riverwalk. Three leaders of this effort and the many volunteers who worked to make it a reality are honored by this bronze sculpture.

Riverwalk Visionaries

Naperville's riverfront was not always the town's crown jewel. For many years, it was a neglected and unsightly spot, a "diamond in the rough," waiting to be discovered. Thanks to the vision of a few residents and the efforts of an entire community, the Riverwalk was lovingly crafted along the West Branch of the DuPage River and dedicated during Naperville's Sesquicentennial celebration in 1981.

Three of the leaders are honored in this bronze sculpture, *Riverwalk Visionaries*, by artist Kathleen Farrell. They are local businessman Jim Moser, architect Chuck George, and Mayor Chet Rybicki. The sculpture also pays tribute to the many volunteers who embraced this project and supported it with their time, special skills, and donations.

Jim Moser, with the help of Chuck George, first envisioned the Riverwalk after meeting to discuss a possible gift that residents could give to the community for the city's 150th birthday. Surprised to discover that the city or park district already owned or controlled a large stretch of the land along the river, they prepared a far-reaching plan to create a linear park near its banks. The park would become a community gathering spot and draw people to the downtown area. Mayor Chet Rybicki, concerned about the economic threat of new shopping centers being built on the outskirts of town, threw the city's support behind the idea. Together the men helped foster a spirit of public/private cooperation that continues to this day.

The sculpture features Jim Moser, his right foot set firmly on an oversized Riverwalk brick, holding architectural drawings from the office of Charles Vincent George in his left hand. Moser's right arm is outstretched, as if pointing out the future location of a covered bridge or shepherd's crook lamppost. Beside him, Mayor Rybicki holds a drawing with relief images of volunteers planting flowers and laying bricks. A photograph of the two community leaders discussing the project was taken by landscape architect Rick Hitchcock in 1981 and served as a historical reference for this sculpture.

Inspired by Andrea del Verrocchio's Italian Renaissance sculpture *Christ and Doubting Thomas* (also known as *Christ and Saint Thomas*), Farrell captures some of the emotional drama of the scene in the poses she creates for the two local men. She also ensures that the sculpture honors the entire community. By placing the logo of Naperville on the mayor's tie, the artist implies that he symbolizes the city. She recognizes all of the volunteers who made the Riverwalk possible, permanently recording their work on the drawing that Rybicki holds in his hands – for the men, women, and children who gave generously of their time were visionaries as well.

Mural
Size: Small individual panels – 24" H x 18" W
Large vinyl mural – 20' H x 100' W

Location
North face of the 35 South
Washington Street building

Dedicated
May 15, 2006

Photo credit: Don Manderscheid

To create this 100-foot-wide mural, viewed from the top of a nearby parking structure, the artists first painted the vignettes in acrylic on a series of small signboards. They then scanned the pictures and dropped the images into a computerized faux architectural scene, ultimately printing the enlarged pictures on vinyl.

#26

Volunteers Welcome

By Ernest Claycomb and Jennifer Richmond

1

2

3

4

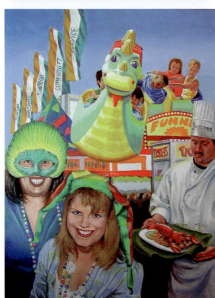

5

6

Photo credits: Friends of Community Public Art

THE ARTISTS

Ernest Claycomb, Muralist, commercial artist, Web designer – Born in Springfield, Illinois, in 1956, Ernest Claycomb received a Bachelor of Fine Arts from the School of the Art Institute of Chicago. He has worked as a painter and graphic artist for more than 30 years and was commissioned to create this mural through the Friends of Community Public Art in Joliet. Claycomb is a skilled commercial artist, muralist, and Web designer.

Jennifer Richmond, Muralist, painter – As an artist with the Friends of Community Public Art in Joliet, Richmond worked with Claycomb to create the series of paintings in this mural. Born in Joliet in 1963, she received a Bachelor of Arts from Governors State University and completed undergraduate and graduate work at Northern Illinois University.

Volunteers Welcome

An incredible spirit of volunteerism flows through Naperville, giving it vitality, creating enduring friendships, and building a strong sense of community. For generations, the commitment of residents to worthy causes has played a major role in making Naperville an exceptional place to live. Volunteers have also reached beyond our nation's borders, and their collective efforts have helped to make the world a better place.

The unusual *Volunteers Welcome* mural, painted by Ernest Claycomb and Jennifer Richmond, recognizes major achievements of seven of the community's most active service organizations.

- The Rotary Club vignette highlights the organization's scholarship program for local students, support of the arts, solar oven projects in poor countries, and major worldwide efforts to eradicate polio.
- The Lions Club panel showcases the club's annual Turkey Trot fund-raiser, its work to provide vision and hearing screening, and its commitment to education.
- The Exchange Club panel features a family and an American flag, sharing the organization's goals to foster the health and growth of strong families, eliminate child abuse, and promote Americanism.
- Scenes from its Mardi Gras Charity Ball, Last Fling, and Lobster Day depict several ways in which the Jaycees raise funds to contribute to various community organizations.
- Pancake Day and Peanut Day, fund-raisers that support the Kiwanis Club's efforts to help numerous local groups, are represented in the fifth panel.
- The illustration for the Naperville Woman's Club highlights its historic Old Stone Church building and its Annual Fine Art Fair.
- Safety Town is the focus of the Naperville Junior Woman's Club volunteer efforts in the final scene, as volunteers work with local police and fire departments to help youngsters learn about safety in a miniature town with small streets and buildings.

To create this mural, the artists first painted the scenes in acrylic on a series of 1½-foot x 2-foot signboards. They then scanned the pictures and dropped the images into a computerized faux architectural scene. The entire illustration was then enlarged and printed on vinyl before the 20' x 100' mural was attached to the building. The original paintings are displayed nearby at eye level.

While most communities welcome visitors with signs that simply display the logos of service organizations, Century Walk chose to announce their presence with this unique mural. A play on words, the name *Volunteers Welcome* implies two messages: "Volunteers welcome you to Naperville!" and "Volunteers are welcome to join us in our efforts to help others."

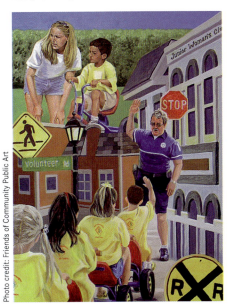

The *Volunteers Welcome* mural highlights the important work and fund-raisers of several Naperville service organizations. The efforts of these and other groups have benefited numerous local, national, and worldwide humanitarian causes.

Mural
Size: 30' H x 75' W

Location
Naperville Community Concert Center in Central Park

Technique
Hand painted on a metal airplane hangar door

Dedicated
June 8, 2006

The Great Concerto mural was painted on an airplane hangar door, shown here as it is opening before the start of a Naperville Municipal Band summer concert.

#27

The Great Concerto

By Barton Gunderson

Photo credit: Don Manderscheid

Barton F. Gunderson, Muralist, sculptor, illustrator, painter – Born in Elmhurst, Illinois, in 1963, Barton Gunderson was hired as an illustrator by the *Chicago Sun-Times* soon after he graduated from high school. Six years later, this self-taught artist presented a large body of his work to McDonald's Corporation and was commissioned to do interior design work for that multinational company. He created a Hollywood-themed mural for the Tokyo McDonald's, and the publicity generated by that artwork captured the attention of Hyatt Hotel Corporation. Gunderson has since completed 27 murals for Hyatt Hotels throughout the United States, as well as 55 murals for The Great American Bagel, 32 murals for McDonald's, and additional artwork for The Athlete's Foot stores, Dayton Hudson, InterContinental Hotels, and Rich Harvest Farms.

In 1992, Gunderson won *Monitor Magazine's* "Design of the Year Award" for The Athlete's Foot flagship store in Los Angeles. Ten years later, he completed a major design project for The News Room restaurant in Minneapolis, and his themed artwork was featured on the Discovery Channel. Vail Resorts has long been a major client of this talented painter, muralist, and sculptor. The resort commissioned the artist to paint portraits of President Gerald Ford, golfing great Greg Norman, and golf designer Tom Fazio. The former Naperville resident now lives near Vail, Colorado.

The Great Concerto

In *The Great Concerto*, muralist Barton Gunderson traces the history of music in downtown Naperville and at this Central Park site. Employing an art deco style greatly influenced by Tamara de Lempicka and Pablo Picasso, Gunderson visually incorporates the movement of music throughout the mural. Like notes in a musical score, the images pulsate across the vast metal canvas, establishing a rhythm of highs and lows and a flow reflective of a conductor's hand.

Similar to other great concertos, this one is composed in three movements – the past, the present, and the future. The mural focuses on the evolution of the Naperville Municipal Band and the participation of a community that has enjoyed musical performances here for more than 150 years.

The composition begins with old Naperville in the upper left corner and with a couple walking down a pathway holding hands. To indicate the passage of time, another couple continues down that path and passes the Central Park gazebo, built for concerts in the 1890s. Near the end of the walkway, exploding cannons ignite memories of the traditional "1812 Overture" performances, which have taken place at each Independence Day concert since 1977.

At center stage is Elmer Koerner, conductor of the municipal band from 1929 to 1965. Band members in period uniforms prepare to play in the original band shell, while the future band director, Ron Keller, waits and watches from the wings.

A vignette at the top right of the mural depicts a community barn dance with residents playing music. A tower lights the stage while people picnic on the lawn below. The scene at the bottom right represents the winter of the last band shell's existence. A trumpeter sounds "Taps" for the fallen band shell, which was replaced in 2003 by the Community Concert Center.

Below the portrait of Elmer Koerner, community members are represented in fine detail, sitting behind emcee Ann Lord at the microphone. As both a tribute to those who attend free band concerts every Thursday evening throughout the summer and as a fund-raiser for the creation of the mural, 51 individuals each paid $1,000 to have a portrait of a family member or friend included in this work. Five additional places were raffled off. The portraits include four of Naperville's mayors, as well as teachers, musicians, and others memorialized in this unique work of art.

As a tribute to loved ones and as a fund-raiser for the creation of the mural, numerous individuals paid to have a portrait of a family member or friend included in this painting (top photo). The close-up in the lower photo demonstrates the rich colors and art deco style of *The Great Concerto*.

The Faces in the Crowd

The fund-raiser that Century Walk held to support the creation of *The Great Concerto* captured the imagination of many local residents. With display ads entitled "Preserve Your Face in Naperville's History," the Century Walk Board encouraged people to "Be a face in the crowd" by paying $1,000 per image to have someone's portrait included in the mural. In response, wives secretly bought portraits of their husbands, who, upon discovering their special gifts, retaliated by purchasing faces of their wives. Adults honored elderly parents, and neighbors recognized their friends. The board added the three living mayors, and the artist included images of band members.

The individual portraits and the people they represent are identified on these two pages.

1. Bruce Webber
2. Terry Szpiech
3. Willard R Smith III
4. Joyce Volpe-Smith
5. Walter Asmus
6. Ralph "Koko" Kokocinski
7. Mary Anne Ostrenga
8. James Ostrenga
9. John Earl Schmitt
10. Frank Glowaty
11. Brian Schultz
12. Jack Smart
13. Arnold Massier
14. Tricia Hummel
15. Walt Fues
16. Karen McCluskey
17. Delores "Dee" Pasternak
18. George Pasternak
19. William Hill
20. Pat Pradel
21. Michelle Springer
22. Thomas O'Donnell
23. Robert Koller
24. Fran Barenbrugge
25. Cindy Barenbrugge
26. Chester Rybicki
27. Margaret "Peg" Price
28. Sam Macrane
29. George Pradel
30. Harris Fawell
31. Ruth Fawell
32. Ann Lord

The Great Concerto (Continued)

33. Gail Niermeyer
34. Don Niermeyer
35. Leslie Girolami
36. Rudy Bilotta
37. Jack Jelinek
38. Joyce Jelinek
39. Brand Bobosky
40. John Hudetz
41. Marge Meyer
42. Tony Meyer
43. David Hummel
44. Bob Van Iten
45. Stanley Weldy
46. Anne Weldy
47. Joel Kolb
48. Sharon Reed
49. Nancy Nyberg
50. Ron Nyberg
51. Leonard Koeder
52. Ray Kinney
53. Norris Yonker
54. Peg Yonker
55. Francois Sebastian Ory
56. Eva Keller Wehrli
57. Adam Keller
58. Florence Schultz
59. Ruth Hamm

Photo credit: Melanie Pusateri

Bronze Sculpture
Size: Five life-size figures on a 2' base

Location
West entrance to Central Park,
Washington Street at Van Buren Avenue

Technique
Lost-wax casting process

Dedicated
November 11, 2006, at 11:11 a.m.

#28
Veterans' Valor
By Shirley McWorter-Moss

Veteran Leo Kuefler (center) proudly wears the Silver Star and Purple Heart he earned during World War II in France. He and Vinnie Mazza were at the dedication of *Veterans' Valor* and were joined by dozens of other veterans.

Photo credits: Don Manderscheid

THE ARTIST

Shirley McWorter-Moss, Sculptor –
Please see McWorter-Moss's biography included with #15, *College, Community, and Country*.

Veterans' Valor

Veterans' Valor honors the heroism of five young men who grew up within a few blocks of each other in Naperville, attended the same schools, and served the country with distinction during World War II. They reflected the values of this small Midwestern town, from which many other young men and women served their nation proudly. Each of the immortalized men returned home safely, decorated with some of America's highest honors for their bravery. Together they earned four Silver Stars, two Distinguished Flying Crosses, and three Purple Hearts.

California artist Shirley McWorter-Moss carefully sculpted each of the men for this memorial, paying great attention to detail. Their jackets, pants, helmets, caps, boots, and straps are authentically re-created, and the various patinas provide a realistic portrayal of their uniforms. She chose to show the soldiers greeting one another informally, beneath the American flag, reuniting as old friends after the war.

On the left is Army 1st Lieutenant Al Rubin, platoon commander, who fought in France. He led a platoon during the invasion of an island off the coast of Normandy, and his unit was the first to capture French soil in the hours before D-Day. This courageous young man returned home with a Silver Star and two Purple Hearts.

Next to him is Army Staff Sergeant Leo Kuefler, tank commander, who saved the lives of his platoon members after his tank and two others were ambushed outside a small French village. Ignoring enemy artillery fire, he ran three-quarters of a mile to help the gunner of a tank that had lost its commander. They continued to fire at enemy positions, leading to the surrender of 18 German soldiers. Kuefler was awarded a Silver Star and Purple Heart.

In the center is Army Air Corps Captain Vinnie Mazza, a B-24 pilot. He took control of his bomber in the skies over Germany after enemy gunners killed his pilot and severely damaged their plane. Mazza finished the bombing run and landed the aircraft safely. For his heroic efforts, he received a Silver Star. After the war, Mazza remained in the Air Force and became a test pilot. He was the first man to test ejection seats and attained the rank of lieutenant colonel.

Reaching out to Mazza in this sculpture is Navy Lieutenant Bob Wehrli, PT boat commander. As a patrol torpedo boat and squadron commander in the Philippines, he earned a Silver Star for leading a close-range attack against Japanese suicide-boat fighters in Batangas Bay.

On the far right is Marine Corps 1st Lieutenant Don Darfler, fighter pilot, who earned a Distinguished Flying Cross flying a Corsair single-engine fighter plane in the Pacific. He earned a second Distinguished Flying Cross as a combat pilot in Korea and later served as a helicopter pilot in Vietnam. Darfler logged more than 15,000 hours of combat flight time during his service to this nation.

Because these men represent the bravery and sacrifices of many others who have served and continue to serve this nation, *Veterans' Valor* is also a tribute to all local men and women who have fought for freedom around the world.

This sculpture was dedicated at 11 minutes after 11:00 a.m. on November 11, 2006 – Veterans Day. Vinnie Mazza and Leo Kuefler, the only surviving veterans depicted in the sculpture, attended the dedication – with hundreds of other visitors, family, and friends. Heralded by music from the Naperville Municipal Band, speeches by dignitaries, and a fly-over by the Lima Lima Flight Team, a letter from our 41st president was read to the crowd. Former President George H. W. Bush wrote in part:

"The men you honor rightly take their place in history's table of glory, for each of them defended the cause of liberty with selflessness and resolve. As a former Navy man and a former Commander in Chief, I join you in saluting the patriots who answered their country's call to duty."

Interactive Kinetic Sculpture
Size: Railroad track – 14' H x 28' W x 13' 6" D
(Approximately 60' of track)
Steam engine – 5' H x 9' 6" W x 2' 6" D
Railway handcar with children –
4' 9" H x 6' W x 2' 6" D
Decorative grasses – Approximately
3' H x 8" W x 8" D with an 18"
counterbalance below the track

Location
DuPage Children's Museum,
301 North Washington Street

Technique
Welded-steel structure with
polyurethane paint
Cut and formed aluminum figures
with cast aluminum details

Dedicated
May 18, 2007

Two children pump the arm of a handcar in this delightful kinetic sculpture.

Photo credit: Jini Clare

#29
Parting the Prairie
By Christine Rojek

Photo credit: Christine Rojek

THE ARTIST

Christine Rojek, Sculptor – Chicago artist Christine Rojek earned a Bachelor of Fine Arts from the University of Illinois at Urbana-Champaign and continued her studies at the American School of Fontainebleau in France where she focused on both performance and installation art. Specializing in public sculpture, Rojek uses the tenets of fine design to create interactive environments that appeal to children and adults alike. These forms of lyrical expression can be provocative, humorous, or whimsical and have become destination pieces in many cities throughout the United States. In addition to *Parting the Prairie* in Naperville, Rojek's sculptures have been installed in six locations in Chicago and 24 nationally. She has received widespread recognition for her achievements, including several fellowship grants from the Illinois Arts Council, the National Endowment for the Arts, and an AT&T Technology in Art Grant. When she is not creating sculpture, Rojek teaches at Columbia College Chicago. She serves on the advisory board for the Center for Art and Architecture and is the co-founder of SculpTours, a touring company that promotes the appreciation and advancement of sculpture in Chicago.

From below, the handcar, young girl, prairie grasses, and train track provide dramatic and vivid images of *Parting the Prairie*.

Parting the Prairie

In this delightful, one-of-a-kind kinetic sculpture, artist Christine Rojek lightheartedly honors the role that trains played in the development of Naperville. Illustrating how locomotives changed the prairie landscape, an aluminum steam engine races along a curved, elevated track, while two young children follow the train on a handcar. Tall hand-formed prairie grasses and native flowers grow along the rails, blowing in the wind.

On the sidewalk below, curious children stop by to turn wheels and push levers, making the sculpture come alive. The train's bell clangs, its brightly painted wheels spin in place along the tracks, and the puppetlike children rhythmically pump the pivoting arm of their handcar.

Each piece of the inventive sculpture was carefully engineered, highlighting the impact of machines on the way people work. The handcar and mechanical figures represent preindustrial, manual labor, while the steam engine transports viewers to modern times. When designing the children, the artist studied antique mechanical metal toys and adapted their movements to the larger puppets. The children's faces were carefully sculpted in Styrofoam and cast in aluminum. Most of the aluminum pieces were cut and formed by hand. Rojek created a counterbalance mechanism to make prairie grasses and flowers sway along the tracks and worked with engineering experts and fabricators to determine the best bearings, pins, shafts, bushings, springs, and support structures for this intricate work of art.

Installed near the entrance to the DuPage Children's Museum, *Parting the Prairie* overlooks the nearby Burlington Northern Santa Fe railroad tracks, accentuating the history lesson portrayed by this sculpture.

The railroad line through Naperville was completed in 1864 and had a major impact on the town's history. After the Great Chicago Fire in 1871, limestone from the local quarries and building materials from the town's tile and brick works were shipped by rail to help rebuild the burned-out city. In the 1880s, the Burlington Railroad built a spur along the DuPage River west of town and created an amusement park called Burlington Park. Its bandstand, racetrack, ball fields, merry-go-round, shooting gallery, and boathouse drew thousands of visitors each weekend during the summer. The role of the railroad grew even stronger when another spur was extended to Jackson Avenue downtown. Railroad cars moved stone from the quarries to the main line and then to other destinations. The locomotives also delivered coal to the downtown coal yard and city power plant where Naperville made its own electricity. Passengers also took advantage of this convenient mode of travel, establishing Naperville as a commuter-friendly city, today only a 30-minute train ride from Chicago.

Bronze Sculpture
Size: 4' 10" H x 4' 3" W x 3' 8" D

Location
East side of Washington Junior High School at 201 North Washington Street

Technique
Lost-wax casting process

Dedicated
May 29, 2007

#30
Officer Friendly
By Sarah Furst

Officer Friendly was a favorite police officer for generations of Naperville children for 29 years, teaching them about safety and helping to establish a playful learning area called Safety Town.

Photo credit: Don Manderscheid

THE ARTIST

Sarah Elizabeth Furst, Sculptor – Born in Midland, Michigan, in 1972, Sarah Furst moved to Naperville when she was in junior high. She studied art at the College of DuPage and earned a Bachelor of Fine Arts from the School of the Art Institute of Chicago. Furst credits the Friends of Community Public Art in Joliet with the significant training she received in life-size bronze sculpting. She enjoys projects that have strong emotive value, especially those that demonstrate the affectionate bond between adults and children.

Sculptor Sarah Furst beautifully portrays the kind and gentle face of *Officer Friendly* and the respectful way he touches the shoulder of a child.

Officer Friendly

Generations of Naperville children grew up with a special friend in the police department. This life-size bronze sculpture, *Officer Friendly*, honors the man who taught youngsters about safety, staying on the right path in life, and personal accountability. Years later, those grown-up children, their parents, and a grateful community rewarded A. George Pradel for his devotion to youth by electing him to four terms as Naperville's mayor.

When he was first hired by the Naperville Police Department in 1966, Officer Pradel asked the chief of police if anyone in the department worked with local school children. Because there were only 14 police officers and limited resources at that time, the answer was no. Pradel then volunteered to go into the schools and talk to the kids on his own time during the day and to work his regular duties on the midnight shift. He developed his own educational curriculum, started a miniature safety town in the Highlands Elementary School parking lot during the summers, and played a leading role in the establishment of the permanent Safety Town operated by the Naperville Junior Woman's Club on Aurora Avenue. Pradel continued his vocation as Officer Friendly for 29 years – until his retirement in 1995.

Sculptor Sarah Furst beautifully portrays the kind and gentle face of *Officer Friendly* looking down at a small girl at Safety Town. The child is going the wrong way on her Big Wheel, and a young crossing guard is holding out his hand, signaling her to stop. The policeman is reaching out to the girl with his left hand while his right hand rests respectfully on the boy's shoulder.

The sculpture is rich in detail, from the badge on the officer's shirt and the keys hanging from his belt to the Safety Town logo on the crossing guard's uniform. Faces, hands, and feet are perfectly formed and tenderly expressive. The little girl's toes curl up in her sandals as she stops her errant vehicle, and the interaction of the three figures demonstrates the warmth of this human connection. Furst masterfully re-creates a moment in time, originally captured in a photograph published in the *Naperville Sun* over 30 years ago.

Pradel views the sculpture as an important lesson of life. "It is about reaching out to young people," he explains. "I think it is incumbent on us as adults to show children the right way. The message is about adults guiding young people and all of us taking care of each other."

Bronze Sculpture
Size: 8' 2" H x 5' 10" W x 7' 3" D sculpture on a 7" H x 4' 2" W x 6' 10" D bronze base

Location
Nichols Library, at southeast corner of Eagle Street and Jefferson Avenue

Technique
Lost-wax casting process

Dedicated
November 12, 2007

#31

The Cat in the Hat

By Leo Rijn

Photo credits: Don Manderscheid

THE ARTISTS

Leo Rijn, Sculptor – Leo Rijn was born in 1954 in Fontana, California. He studied sculpting at Long Beach State in California and began his successful art career in the entertainment industry, creating props for Disney's theme parks. He later worked as a set sculptor for numerous Hollywood film productions and as a character designer for film.

This artist was selected to create the Dr. Seuss sculptures because of his prized accomplishments with some of today's top talent in the world of film, entertainment, and the visual arts, including work with Tim Burton, Ang Lee, and Steven Spielberg. Rijn was the lead artist for many of the sculptured characters and buildings at Seuss Landing, part of Universal Studios' Islands of Adventure amusement park in Orlando, Florida. He was identified as one of today's brightest sculpting talents because of his ability to breathe life into the written word and successfully transform two-dimensional ideas into three-dimensional works of art. Due to his successful history with Dr. Seuss characters, Chase Art Companies in Northbrook, Illinois, selected Rijn to be the inaugural sculptor for their Dr. Seuss Tribute Collection.

Dr. Seuss (Theodor Seuss Geisel), Writer, illustrator, cartoonist, sculptor, and painter –
Please see Geisel's biography included with #32, *Green Eggs and Ham*.

These illustrations by Theodor Seuss Geisel for his book *The Cat in the Hat* announce the cat's uninvited entrance into the children's world.

The Cat in the Hat

We looked!
Then we saw him step in on the mat!
We looked!
And we saw him!
The Cat in the Hat!

While reading these words, generations of children have taken their first peek at the mischievous and uninvited magical feline that turned a fictional household upside down and changed children's literature forever. Following the enormously successful publication of Dr. Seuss's *The Cat in the Hat* in 1957, Random House created a special division, Beginner Books, to add zest and imagination to books that would encourage children to read. The publishing house, which had published all of the author's books since 1937, named Dr. Seuss – Theodor Seuss Geisel – as the first president of its new division.

On the 50th anniversary of the book's release, Century Walk purchased one of nine monumental sculptures of *The Cat in the Hat* from the Dr. Seuss Tribute Collection. Installed outside Nichols Library in downtown Naperville, it is one of only two monument-sized *The Cat in the Hat* sculptures that have been placed in public settings. To date, all others from this edition are in private collections. When the *Green Eggs and Ham* sculpture was created in 2009, Century Walk once again purchased one of the nine limited-edition sculptures of the book's main character, Sam-I-Am, and placed it at the 95th Street Library in the southern part of town. As a nationally recognized "kid friendly" community known for its outstanding schools and award-winning public libraries, Naperville is an ideal setting for these sculptures that represent children's love of reading.

Permission to create this and other sculptures of Dr. Seuss characters was given to Chase Art Companies by the Geisel estate. The cleverly crafted bronze artwork of *The Cat in the Hat* captures the first image that readers see of the cat, stepping on the mat, entering the home of two small children on a rainy day.

The sculpture itself was created by Leo Rijn who was selected by Chase Art Companies because of his outstanding work as the lead artist for Seuss Landing at Universal Studios in Orlando, Florida. Ultimately, Rijn will create eight Dr. Seuss sculptures portraying characters from Geisel's books. The Dr. Seuss Tribute Collection I will include *The Cat in the Hat*, *Green Eggs and Ham*, *Yertle the Turtle*, and *Horton the Elephant*.

Bronze Sculpture
Size: 138" H x 52" W x 87" D

Location
95th Street Library, 3015 Cedar Glade Drive

Technique
Lost-wax casting process

Dedicated
March 6, 2009

#32

Green Eggs and Ham

By Leo Rijn

Theodor Seuss Geisel wrote and illustrated 44 children's books during his career. He brought imagination and zest to books that encouraged children to read and changed children's literature forever.

Photo credits: Don Manderscheid

THE ARTISTS

Dr. Seuss (Theodor Seuss Geisel), Writer, illustrator, cartoonist, sculptor, and painter – During his career, Geisel wrote and illustrated 44 children's books – including such favorites as *The Cat in the Hat* (1957); *Green Eggs and Ham* (1960); *One Fish Two Fish Red Fish Blue Fish* (1960); *How the Grinch Stole Christmas!* (1957), and *Oh, the Places You'll Go!* (1990). His books have been translated into more than 25 languages, and some were made into movies or television specials. More than 200 million of Geisel's books sold during his lifetime, and an additional 250 million Dr. Seuss books have been sold since his death in 1991.

While best known for writing and illustrating children's books with fanciful rhymes, hard-to-pronounce names, and strange-looking characters, Geisel lived a life as colorful as his books. Born in Springfield, Massachusetts, in 1904, he was the son of a brewmaster who became a zookeeper during the Prohibition Era. Young Ted's father brought home strange horns, beaks, and body parts from dead zoo animals, feeding the boy's imagination and planting the seeds for his later works of art. His mother taught him to rhyme, and he taught himself to draw. After graduating from Dartmouth and briefly attending Oxford, he began a successful career as an editorial cartoonist, satirist, and illustrator. He created winning advertising campaigns for the Standard Oil Company, introducing his own brand of humor into the series of "Quick, Henry, the Flit!" cartoons. Seuss wrote his first children's book, *And to Think That I Saw It on Mulberry Street*, in 1937. It was rejected by 28 publishing houses before Vanguard Press agreed to take a chance on the artist-illustrator's inventive style.

Seuss earned numerous accolades during his lifetime. He won Academy Awards for two documentaries that he wrote during World War II while under the command of Colonel Frank Capra, the legendary Hollywood director. During the 1970s and 1980s, he won Peabody and Emmy Awards for his television specials, and, in 1984, he received a Pulitzer Prize.

After Geisel's death, the public was invited to view "the secret art" of Dr. Seuss, a collection of delightful watercolors, oils, acrylics, and multimedia "unorthodox taxidermy" sculptures – many sporting the unusual horns, antlers, and beaks that his father had given him when he was a child. His works now appear in art galleries and museums throughout the country, sharing the spotlight with works of other great artists.

Leo Rijn, Sculptor –
Please see Rijn's biography included with #31, *Cat in the Hat*.

Green Eggs and Ham

Green Eggs and Ham, one of the all-time bestselling children's books in the English language, is the subject of the second sculpture in the Dr. Seuss Tribute Collection. Once again, Century Walk purchased one of nine limited edition monumental sculptures and included it in the community's public art program. It is the only monument-sized *Green Eggs and Ham* sculpture currently available on public view.

This playful sculpture features the book's main character, Sam-I-Am, balancing his platter of green eggs and ham on a gloved stick above his head. Dr. Seuss wrote *Green Eggs and Ham* after his publisher at Random House, Bennett Cerf, bet him $50 that he could not write a book with a vocabulary of only 50 words. Seuss won the wager.

While *The Cat in the Hat* was the first Century Walk piece of art that was not a depiction of Naperville's past, *Green Eggs and Ham* was the first to be located outside of Naperville's downtown area. These two sculptures mark the beginning of phase two of Century Walk and dramatically showcase the program's evolution. What was initially a downtown walk highlighting the city's history is now an expanded public art program that includes unlimited subjects and the placement of artwork throughout the community.

The *Green Eggs and Ham* sculpture from the Dr. Seuss Tribute Collection captures Sam-I-Am, balancing his platter of green eggs and ham on a gloved stick above his head, similar to this illustration from Dr. Seuss's popular book.

Copper Sculpture
Size: 6½' H x 3' W x 40" D

Location
Along the Riverwalk, northeast of the Moser Tower and Millennium Carillon

Technique
Lost-wax casting process

Dedicated
May 3, 2009

Artist Bart Gunderson, who also created *The Great Concerto* mural, posed next to *Mr. and Mrs. Naperville* after the sculpture's dedication.

#33
Mr. and Mrs. Naperville
By Barton Gunderson

Photo credits: Don Manderscheid

THE ARTIST
Barton F. Gunderson, Sculptor, muralist, illustrator, and painter –
Please see Gunderson's biography with #27, *The Great Concerto*.

Mr. and Mrs. Naperville

Within footsteps of the carillon tower named in their honor, a bronze sculpture pays tribute to one of Naperville's most influential couples, Harold and Margaret Moser. Devoted to each other and to the community, they left a twentieth-century legacy of entrepreneurship and philanthropy that changed the local landscape forever.

In a lifetime punctuated with debilitating illness, Harold Moser overcame immense obstacles as a young man to fulfill his destiny as a successful businessman and community leader. Moser's teenage dream of becoming a priest ended on a basketball court at St. Lawrence Academy when an injury resulted in a bone infection that nearly cost him his life. After returning home from that Wisconsin school, he eventually recovered, graduated from Naperville High School in 1933, and attended North Central College where he worked as an editor on the school paper. Moser's formal education ended when he completed his sophomore year. With the financial backing of his father and his own experience as a journalist, in 1935 he established a new newspaper in town – the *Naperville Sun*. A year later, he sold the newspaper to Harold White and Gordon Haist.

Moser held a number of temporary jobs throughout the remainder of the Great Depression but suffered another serious bout of osteomyelitis in 1940, which permanently stiffened his hips. To ensure that his son would become a productive citizen, Harold's father purchased a local coal yard in 1941 and put the young man in charge of its operations. Harold quickly recognized that oil and gas would soon replace coal. He also envisioned the strong building industry that would emerge when the war ended, so he strategically phased out the coal business and stocked the yard with lumber. By 1946, he established Moser Lumber Company, began purchasing neighboring farmland, and started building homes. In 1960, he founded Macom Corporation, which would eventually develop over one-third of the homesites in Naperville and more than 25 of its subdivisions.

Harold and Margaret Moser lived a humble, faith-filled life and believed in sharing their good fortune with the community. These civic leaders donated land to four of the town's Catholic churches, gave $1 million toward the construction of the Millennium Carillon, generously supported North Central College and Benedictine University, and contributed to many other local causes. Happily married for 52 years, Harold and Margaret died within a week of each other in December of 2001.

In the copper sculpture *Mr. and Mrs. Naperville*, artist Barton Gunderson depicts the self-made man and his wife breaking ground for a new development while holding on to some of the things they hold dear – the city of Naperville, Saints Peter and Paul Church, North Central College, and the neighborhoods they helped create. They are being chiseled out of a rock that symbolizes their strong foundations and the strength they share with each other. Like the town of Naperville that is still being developed, the figures of Harold and Margaret Moser are unfinished. Their faces, hands, and torsos are polished and refined, but their lower bodies are yet to emerge. The roughly sculpted surfaces of the unchiseled rock symbolize the development, innovation, and challenges that remain for the growing community.

Mural
Size: 67' W x 12' H with 14' peaks

Location
South wall of the Naperville Fine Arts Center and Gallery, 508 North Center Street

Technique
Humorous illustration with realistic elements, hand painted with oil-based sign enamel on primed Dryvit-clad walls

Dedicated
August 25, 2009

#34

World's Greatest Artists
By Mike Venezia and Marianne Lisson Kuhn

Mike Venezia and guest artist Faith Ringgold stand in front of a favorite mural scene during the dedication of the *World's Greatest Artists*. The vignette shows Cassie Lightfoot, one of Ringgold's story-quilt characters, soaring above New York City with the George Washington Bridge in the background.

Photo credit: Jini Clare

Photo credit: Don Manderscheid

THE ARTISTS

Mike Venezia, Mural creator and designer – Born in New York City in 1945, Venezia moved to the Chicago area with his family when he was 10 years old. He has wonderful childhood memories of sketching airplanes and battle scenes with his father. Mike continued drawing throughout elementary and high school, frequently using his art to complete special assignments. He later attended the School of the Art Institute of Chicago where he earned a Bachelor of Fine Arts degree. Venezia served as executive art director and vice president at Leo Burnett Company, Chicago's largest advertising agency, for 33 years. In 1978, he also began a writing career when he started to author and illustrate books for Children's Press. Prompted by his humorous artistic talents and his knowledge of art history, he convinced the editors at Children's Press to publish a series of books for children about the great artists of the world. Today, *Getting to Know the World's Greatest Artists* is the #1 best-selling trade book series for Children's Press and a top seller in school and library sales. Venezia works out of his home in Glen Ellyn, Illinois.

Marianne Lisson Kuhn, Muralist – The Century Walk board and artist Mike Venezia selected Marianne Lisson Kuhn to hand paint the *World's Greatest Artists* mural because of the fine work she had done creating Century Walk's 2005 mural, *The Way We Were*. Please see Kuhn's biography with #24, *The Way We Were*.

The personalities and artworks of 32 internationally renowned and two local artists are featured in this imaginative mural. In the two photos above, readers can find Michelangelo, Vincent van Gogh, Georges Seurat, Pablo Picasso, Dick Locher, Grant Wood, and their works of art.

World's Greatest Artists

This imaginative mural, *World's Greatest Artists*, captivates viewers with its humorous style, educates them about the lives and works of famous artists, and motivates them to learn more about the history of art. Appropriately painted on the side of the Naperville Fine Arts Center and Gallery, this intriguing mural highlights the personalities and famous works of 32 internationally renowned and two local artists.

From Michelangelo painting the ceiling of the Sistine Chapel to Jackson Pollock flinging a can of paint, the vibrant composition pulls people of all ages into its delightful tableau. Alexander Calder sits on one of his mobiles. Salvador Dalí holds a brush with his flamboyant waxed mustache while painting a melting clock. Diego Rivera, wearing a bandana and a bandolier stuffed with tubes of paint, works on a portrait of his wife, Frida Kahlo. Faith Ringgold proves that "anyone can fly" as one of her story-quilt characters, Cassie Lightfoot, soars above New York City with the George Washington Bridge visible in the background. Inquisitive eyes can also find Leonardo da Vinci, Georgia O'Keeffe, Rembrandt van Rijn, Toulouse-Lautrec, Andy Warhol, Vincent van Gogh, Georges Seurat, Pablo Picasso, Grant Wood, Paul Gauguin, René Magritte, Claude Monet, Mary Cassatt, and many others. A special feature of the mural is the illustration of Dick Tracy, showcasing the legendary detective's profile and yellow fedora. Tracy was personally painted on the mural and autographed by famous Naperville cartoonist Dick Locher, who originally was an assistant to the comic strip creator, Chester Gould, and has illustrated the comic strip since 1983.

Painted by Marianne Lisson Kuhn, the mural's design was the inspiration of Glen Ellyn artist Mike Venezia who is the author/illustrator of a series of children's books, *Getting to Know the World's Greatest Artists*. Also a member of the Naperville Art League, headquartered in the Naperville Fine Arts Center and Gallery, Venezia wanted to create a piece that would become a celebration of great art. The mural has also become the first delightful stepping stone for schoolchildren and others who want to wade into the vast pool of art that exists in museums throughout the Chicagoland area.

Bronze Sculpture
Size: 8½' H x 6½' W x 4' 10" D, 1 ton

Location
Along the Riverwalk, between the Naperville Township building and the nearby covered bridge

Technique
Lost-wax casting process

Dedicated
April 11, 2010

Two Riverwalk visitors study the *Dick Tracy* sculpture while relaxing on one of the benches nearby.

#35
Dick Tracy
By Dick Locher and Donald L. Reed

Photo credit: Don Manderscheid

Photo credits: Jini Clare

THE ARTISTS

Dick Locher, Cartoonist, sculptor, painter – Winner of the 1983 Pulitzer Prize for Editorial Cartooning and numerous other awards, Dick Locher's ability to capture the absurdities of life through political cartooning is known worldwide. This Naperville resident established his reputation as one of the world's leading editorial cartoonists at the *Chicago Tribune*, where he has worked since 1973. His cartoons are nationally syndicated by Tribune Media Services and have been reprinted in many of the nation's major magazines and throughout the world.

Born in 1929 in Dubuque, Iowa, Locher graduated from Loras Academy and later studied art at the University of Iowa. He earned degrees from the Chicago Academy of Fine Arts in 1951 and the Los Angeles Art Center School in 1955. Locher served in the U.S. Air Force during the Korean War, attaining the rank of captain.

Although he is best known for his cartoons, Locher is an accomplished fine-art painter and sculptor. He has also published several books, including *Dick Locher Draws Fire, Send in the Clowns, The Daze of Whine and Neurosis*, and several others.

In addition to receiving the Pulitzer Prize, Locher has been awarded the National Cartoonist Society's Silver T-Square Award for Lifetime Achievement (2006), the John Fischetti Editorial Cartooning Award (1987), the Peter Lisagor Award (1985, 1990, 1991, 1992), the Illinois FBI Man of the Year Award (1996), and numerous other honors. In 1986, with members of the American Association of Editorial Cartoonists, he founded the John Locher Memorial Award. This contest not only honors the memory of Locher's son, but it also helps discover and help aspiring cartoonists.

Locher is affectionately regarded in Naperville, where his sense of humor and involvement with charitable organizations grace the community.

Donald L. Reed, Sculptor – Don Reed has worked with Dick Locher for over 30 years and welcomed the opportunity to collaborate with him in the creation of the monumental Dick Tracy sculpture. The chief sculptor at River's Edge Foundry, LLC in Beloit, Wisconsin, Reed has an extensive art background, including study at the Sorbonne. In August of 2009, Reed's life-size sculpture of President Ronald Reagan on horseback, entitled *Begins the Trail*, was dedicated at Heritage Crossing Riverfront Plaza in Dixon, Illinois. Many of his bronze and silver sculptures can be found in museums, corporate buildings, fine art galleries, and private collections throughout the world.

Artist Dick Locher (top photo) captured *Dick Tracy's* arrival while wearing a jacket with the crime fighter's famous face and yellow fedora.

Dick Tracy

Larger than life, the towering crime-fighting legend *Dick Tracy* stands under a streetlight and watches over the Riverwalk, keeping visitors safe from harm. Speaking into his two-way wrist radio with his yellow overcoat blowing in the wind, the internationally known hero makes sure that crime doesn't pay and that all villains are brought to justice.

Renowned local artist Dick Locher created the original 11-inch-tall clay maquette of *Dick Tracy* for Century Walk. Locher then worked with Donald Reed to transform the artwork into this dramatic almost nine-foot high monumental sculpture. Special patinas were applied to the bronze piece to capture Tracy's trademark yellow fedora and overcoat and colorful tie. Permission to re-create the cartoon legend was granted to Century Walk Corporation by Tribune Media Services, Inc.

The *Dick Tracy* comic strip was created by the late Chester Gould. First appearing on October 4, 1931, in the Detroit *Mirror*, the strip was soon distributed by the Chicago Tribune Syndicate throughout the United States. Gould, who lived in Woodstock, Illinois, wrote and illustrated *Dick Tracy* until his retirement on December 25, 1977. Naperville resident and *Chicago Tribune* editorial cartoonist Dick Locher assisted Gould on the strip from 1957 to 1961, working closely with the famous artist and developing a fun-filled personal relationship with him. Locher has been the artist of the *Dick Tracy* comic strip since 1983 and, in 2005, took over as both writer and artist. Artist Jim Brozman now assists Locher with the strip, ensuring that this iconic detective will live on in the annals of justice. More than 12.5 million readers throughout the world follow this pop culture hero each day.

Naperville has been Dick Tracy's "headquarters" since 1983, making the Riverwalk an especially appropriate home for this signature Century Walk piece. The artwork is one of only a handful of sculptures honoring historic cartoon strip characters in the United States and preserves a unique piece of Americana.

#	Title	#	Title
1	*Naperville's Own*	18	*Be the Best That You Can Be*
2	*The Printed Word*	19	*Spirit of the American Doughboy*
3	*River Reveries*	20	*Yes We Can!*
4	*Heartland Harvest*	21	*Lean on US*
5	*Growth and Change*	22	*Symbiotic Sojourn*
6	*A City in Transit*	23	*Two in a Million*
7	*Naperville*	24	*The Way We Were*
8	*Man's Search for Knowledge through the Ages*	25	*Riverwalk Visionaries*
9	*Reading Children*	26	*Volunteers Welcome*
10	*Genevieve*	27	*The Great Concerto*
11	*River of Life*	28	*Veterans' Valor*
12	*Golden Rule Days*	29	*Parting the Prairie*
13	*Pillars of the Community*	30	*Officer Friendly*
14	*Horse Market Days*	31	*The Cat in the Hat*
15	*College, Community and Country*	32	*Green Eggs and Ham*
16	*Cars of the Century*	33	*Mr. and Mrs. Naperville*
17	*A Lifetime Together*	34	*World's Greatest Artists*
		35	*Dick Tracy*

the locations

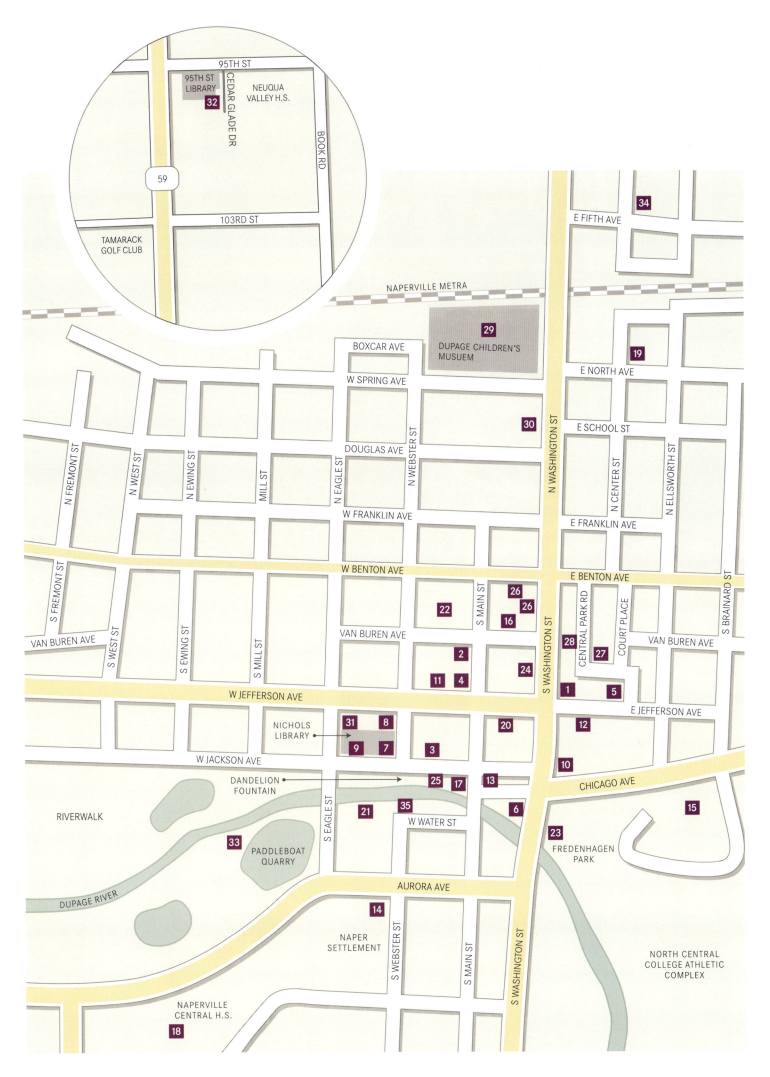

Photo credit: *Daily Herald*, Tanit Jarusan, Photographer
(This photo was reprinted by permission of the *Daily Herald*, Arlington Heights, IL.)

techniques

The Process of Creating Murals

The following information and photographs were provided by Barton Gunderson, muralist.

Most murals are created using the same basic steps that this artist used in painting *The Great Concerto*, although the types of paints and tools may differ.

1. **A small drawing of the mural is created.**

    The size of Gunderson's initial drawing was 35" wide by 15" tall.

2. **The surface is prepared.**

    The Great Concerto was painted on a metal airplane hangar door. To sustain the longevity of the mural, the artist first prepped the door with high polymer acrylics that sealed the aluminum.

3. **Background colors are painted.**

    Gunderson laid out flat layers of acrylic paint to create the background colors. He used a spray gun to cover the 2,250-square-foot surface.

4. **Details of the composition are sketched over the background colors.**

    While projection of the initial drawing onto the final surface is often the first choice of artists, Gunderson decided to freehand the entire mural due to lighting concerns and the large size of the door.

5. **The details of the mural are painted.**

    Using a ½-inch brush to paint most of the mural, Gunderson spent over 1,700 hours and 14 gallons of pure acrylic polymer archival museum-quality color to complete this magnificent history of music in downtown Naperville.

6. **The finished artwork is sealed.**

    When Gunderson completed painting *The Great Concerto*, he clear coated the entire mural with museum-quality, 100 percent acrylic nonyellowing UVA/UVB protectants.

The Casting Process
The "Lost-Wax Method"

Sculptor and foundry owner Jeff Adams shared the following information about the lost-wax casting process. All bronze sculptures are created using these basic steps.

1. A clay model is created.

2. A flexible rubber mold with a rigid backing (called the "mother mold") is made from the clay original.

3. Hot wax is poured into the rubber mold to get a wax duplicate of the original clay.

4. The wax pattern is repeatedly dipped into a ceramic slurry to create a ceramic mold around the wax.

5. The ceramic mold is fired to 1,600 degrees Fahrenheit to remove all the wax from inside.

6. Bronze is melted at approximately 2,000 degrees Fahrenheit and poured into the ceramic mold.

7. The ceramic mold is broken off to reveal the bronze casting. Now the work begins.

8. Sprues and gates are cut and ground off, and casting imperfections are fixed. Pieces are welded back together and sandblasted to prepare for patination.

9. A patina finish is applied using heat and various chemicals to oxidize the surface of the metal.

© by Jeff Adams, sculptor,
inBronze Studio/Gallery/Foundry
Reprinted with permission.

The Process of Creating Mosaics

The following information and photographs were provided by mosaic artist Jennifer Hereth and Thomas Vangel Photography.

1. The design of the mosaic is created.

    It can be drawn on the surface that will display the artwork or on a sheet of paper that can be moved to the artwork's final location.

2. Tools are assembled and materials are prepared.

    Pieces of tile, plates, cups, buttons, glass, marble, or other materials are broken or cut for placement in the mosaic. This is a memorable way to reuse chipped or broken china.

3. The pieces, called *tessarae*, are glued in place.

    Hereth recommends leaving ¼-inch to ⅓-inch spaces between the individual tiles. This allows the grout to show and become part of the design. Careful attention is given to the edges of glass or ceramic, ensuring that the final mosaic has no sharp or cutting surfaces.

4. Grout is mixed.

    Tints and any necessary additives are mixed into the grout.

5. Grout is spread over small sections of the mosaic like frosting, completely covering the tiles and the spaces between them.

6. After the grout is set, but before it is completely dry, the tiles are wiped clean with a wet sponge or Q-Tip.

Century Walk Corporation
Board of Directors' Acknowledgments

In the Beginning – Fostered by a fundamentally sound concept, a community sensitive to its heritage, and a vision of what was possible, an initial group of interested parties was formed in 1995 to investigate a request from the Central Area Naperville Development Organization (CANDO) to learn if public art was desirable for the community.

The early committee meetings provided more questions than answers. After all, something like this was not only in the eye of the beholder but taxpayer as well. Early letters to the editor were critical of the exploratory endeavor. But persistence mixed with patience allowed the project to convince many that maybe it should be given a try. The following committee members laid the ground work to proceed: Greg Asimakoupoulos, Mary Ann Bobosky, Ed Channell, Jini Clare, Hal Dickson, Barbara Dwyer, Glen Ekey, Bill Esser, Timm Etters, Joanne Ford, Cynthia Foyles, Peggy Frank, Charles George, Joseph Ghaben, Angela Graefenhain, Larry Gregory, Debbie Grinnell, Kris Guill, Bart Gunderson, Lynn Harrison, Dave Hartin, Rita Harvard, Elizabeth Heavener, Sally Hewlett, Rick Hitchcock, Court Kenaston, Barbara Knuckles, Sue Koranda, Bill Kottmann, Pierre Lebeau, Paul Lehman, Corrine Matts, Julie McCutcheon, Chuck D. Mesigh, Ron Miller, Dee Pasternak, Dorcas Pearcy, Cindy Pepple, Lou Petritz, Veronica Porter, Dan Racz, Ken Ross, Alfred Rubin, Sandy Shamburek, Mike Skarr, Stacy Slack, Mary Kay Slocumb, Chris Smith, Christy Sweet, James Tezak, Bettye Wehrli, Sue Wehrli, Leslie Wilson, Doris Wood, and Dwight Yackley.

Then local State Senator Christopher Lauzen provided an introduction to Illinois Arts Council Executive Director Lori Spear Montana, which ultimately resulted in a $10,000 award and a great deal of credibility. The Naperville Art League made a donation of $1,000, which began a long-standing informal partnership that still exists today. Most of 1995 was spent familiarizing the community at large with the fledgling public art program.

The Power of the Press – Perhaps the outside influence that had the greatest effect in the beginning and throughout the years was the printed media, principally the *Naperville Sun*, the *Daily Herald*, and *Positively Naperville* – in particular its publisher and editor, Stephanie Penick. Without their favorable accounts of what Century Walk was trying to accomplish, more than likely we would never have accomplished anything.

The Council Comes to the Rescue – With this positive media coverage, it was time to solicit our city council's vote up or down on financial funding. Property owners or their representatives, such as Joseph K. Ghaben, A. Louis Petritz, James J. Tezak, and Dwight Yackley; public and civic organizations, including Illinois Arts Council Foundation, Naperville Art League, Illinois State Museum Lockport Gallery, Naperville Community Unit School District 203, Naperville Heritage Society, Central Area Naperville Development Organization, Rotary Club of Naperville, and North Central College, and citizens of all ages like Frank Allston, Greg Asimakoupoulos, JoAnn Martin Baumgartner, Barbara B. Dwyer, Glen A. Ekey, Scott R. Etters, Timm Etters, Sally Hewlett, Charles D. Mesigh, Christy Sweet, and Rachel Taylor rallied and signed a formal project proposal gratuitously prepared by Rick Hitchcock of Hitchcock Design Group, Inc. and printed by Minuteman Press in Naperville, courtesy of Ray Kinney.

The council saw the cultural value of what could result from the proposal, as well as the downside if the naysayers proved to be correct. Consequently, $30,000 was awarded by increasing the existing hotel tax 6 percent with an annual sunset provision requiring us to perform, or there wouldn't be a second year. This initial funding allowed us to complete the first three pieces of art: a relief sculpture named *Naperville's Own*, a mural entitled *The Printed Word*, and two mosaic benches, *River Reveries*.

Repeat Performance – Buoyed by the community's initial acceptance of our public art, we were determined to pursue our goals and establish an important outdoor gallery of significant pieces. In retrospect, the second year was probably the most critical to the success of the project. The selection of our first abstract sculpture (*Growth and Change*), a mammoth mural (*A City in Transit*), and a tile mosaic (*Heartland Harvest*) proved to be prophetic. The growing art collection displayed the variety and value of our melding public art with history: art available in public places, free every minute, all day, every day.

Century Walk Corporation
Board of Directors' Acknowledgments (Continued)

Public Art Meets Public Library – As important as the second year was, another fateful occurrence was the inclusion of existing public art situated at Nichols Library that had been donated by private citizens to the library in the mid-1980s. The transfer of ownership from the library board headed by Carolyn S. Roscich in 1998 enabled our fledgling public art project to dramatically increase in size, by three exhibits to nine, without the expenditure of development dollars.

The Future of Phase II – Even as our thirtieth piece of artwork was installed in 2007, fulfilling our original vision, the community has continued its support of "Phase II" of our effort. With a slightly revised mission, Century Walk has expanded its scope to include pieces that do not necessarily represent Naperville's twentieth-century history and to allow for the placement of art at parks, schools, and private properties anywhere within corporate boundaries. We believe future expansion throughout the community, consistent with our long-range mission statement, will add to our impressive gallery of public art that we have only just begun. *We hope you, the reader, whether a history buff or art aficionado, will agree!*

Special Events and Cultural Amenities Fund – We are especially grateful to the City of Naperville and local taxpayers who made Century Walk and this book possible with significant grants throughout the years from the Special Events and Cultural Amenities Fund (SECA).

Our Thanks Go To – Jini Clare of Clare Communications who so carefully tended to the daunting task of revealing Century Walk's artists and their art in this book, Carolyn Gerard of Gerard Design and design team members Lisa Johnson and Jack Jacobi for beautifully laying out the pages, Merrie Ann Nall for her editing expertise, and RR Donnelley for printing this polished and professional collector's edition for readers to enjoy throughout this century and beyond.

We also want to express our gratitude to numerous individuals, property owners, businesses, and organizations that have contributed for more than 15 years to Century Walk's success, particularly our Naperville City Council and Managers*: Jim Boyajian, Judith Brodhead, Peter T. Burchard*, Joe Dunn, Mary L. Ellingson, David R. Fiore, Richard R. Furstenau, Kevin M. Gallagher, Paul Hinterlong, Doug Krause, Doug Krieger*, Samuel T. Macrane, Kenn Miller, Ronald Miller*, Mayor A. George Pradel, Margaret P. Price, John Rosanova, Darlene Senger, James L. Sidall, Gary von Berhren, and Grant Wehrli.

We hereby acknowledge those who played a significant role, recognizing that we can't do so for everyone and apologizing to those whom we inadvertently fail to mention. We'll now chronologically reference these volunteers with their respective participation associated with numbered artworks (1-35).

1996: Century Walk would never have happened without the support of our first three property owners: Firstar Bank (1), the *Naperville Sun* (2), and the renovated Jackson Avenue city hall (3), as well as the principals responsible for such participation: Lou Petriz, Jim Tezak, and Joe Ghaben, respectively. Debbie Grinnell from Naper Settlement supplied essential background information for the mosaic benches, Director Ron Keller and the Naperville Municipal Band played for each dedication, and Timm Etters of Odyssey Creations, Inc. designed our timeless logo.

Equally important that first year were the plaques explaining the art donated by Firstar Bank (1), Harris Bank (2), and MidAmerica Bank (3). In subsequent years, MidAmerica also sponsored plaques at locations (4), (5), (6), and (13). In addition, we are truly grateful to those plaque providers who subsequently stepped up: Bridgeview Bank Group (11), Harris Bank (7), (8), (9), and (20), Mustang Construction, Inc. (15), Naperville Evening Kiwanis (12), Stephen J. Subach, Sr. (23), and Dwight and Ruth Yackley (22).

1997: This year saw the first wave of volunteers assisting in producing the art. McKenna Tile Company grouted *Heartland Harvest* (4) on the building owned by Ken and Nancy Ross after the volunteers helped cut tiles and lay the *tesserae*. These volunteers included: Helen Aiken, Carla Bryant, Carla Carr, Don Castro, Jennifer Cox, Karen Keene Day, Jan Dusek, Dottie Farrell, Carolyn Finzer, Deirdre Finzer, Nicole Finzer, Kim Frieders, Raye Isenberg, Erin Jordan, Kathy Knapp, Jerome Kugel, Julie Kulak, Kevin Kulak, Dennis Legut, Caroline Marcinkowski, Alison McSherry, Elaine Reuttiger, Willard Smith, Mira Weisenthal, and Jeanne Zimmerman. The farm families included in the border surrounding the mosaic were selected by fifth/sixth-generation Napervillians, including Gene and Sharon Drendel, Wilbert and Ruth Hageman, and Ray and Harriet Kuhn.

Still more volunteers, including Blake Bobosky, the Mel Finzer family, Carol Graves, Kristin Guill, John Guill, Alan Juranek, Jerry Juranek, Joseph Juranek, Jean Leverenz, and Gary von Behren, supplied twentieth-century tools for *Growth and Change* (5) at the Jefferson Hill Shops owned by the Guills. To paint the mammoth mural *City in Transit* (6) at The Lantern, owned by Don and Pat Feldott, Sound Incorporated President Ed Channell provided the scaffold lift.

1998: As indicated above, the Naperville Public Library Board transferred three works of existing art at Nichols Library, (7), (8), and (9), to Century Walk, bringing our total to nine.

The Gil Ellman family also came forth, volunteering their music store's north face, when *The Printed Word* (2) needed to be re-created and relocated.

This was also the year that Willard R Smith III, known as "Will," joined our board and volunteered to use his art background to be our "conservator." For 12 years he has capably repaired, replaced, or repainted weathered or damaged tile, glass, ceramic, and painted surfaces.

Century Walk Corporation
Board of Directors' Acknowledgments (Continued)

1999: Property owners Dwight and Ruth Yackley of BBM, Inc. not only donated their property for *Genevieve* (10), but they also cosponsored with the *Naperville Sun* a fifth printing of Genevieve Towsley's book, *A View of Historic Naperville*. Eleven years later, they sponsored the printing of the first edition of *Century Walk: Art Imitating History*.

Another couple, Arie and Sharon Hoogendoorn, provided the setting for the *River of Life* (11), which received funding from A.R.T. Studio Clay Co., Japanese Chamber of Commerce and Industry of Chicago, Jones Intercable, Inc., Marshall Field Foundation, Naperville Education Foundation, and the Naperville Jaycees. The students were guided by educators Noel Anderson, Judy Dagenais, Kay Dostal, Grace Frejlach-Grubb, Nora Howe, Corinne Peterson, Ellen Rathunde, Ross Rutherford, Stacy Slack, Elizabeth Smith, and Bill Vose.

These two additions were included in our third brochure featuring eleven locations and printed courtesy of Harris Bank, as were the first two in 1996 and 1998. Subsequently, Harris Bank has partnered with the *Daily Herald* in printing thousands of brochures of our expanding art in 2002, 2004, and 2007 presenting 16, 22, and 30 completed artworks, respectively.

2000: The First Church of Christ, Scientist, provided the inspiration for *Golden Rule Days* (12) and Mike and Mary Phillips provided the property. The Indiana one-room schoolhouse bell was donated by Dr. Arlo Schilling, retired president of North Central College. Packer Engineering, Inc. donated the electrical mechanism necessary to ring the bell three times daily. Subsequently, Yorktown Center, Inc. donated a bench honoring the artist couple, George and Shirley Olson.

2001: The Jack Horsley family and their tenant, Sullivan's Steakhouse, managed by Zaidi Syed, provided the opportunity to create *Pillars of the Community* (13).

The City of Naperville, via the Naperville Heritage Society and Naperville Settlement, spearheaded by Peggy Frank, arranged for the placement of *Horse Market Days* (14). The plaque was given in memory of Phillip Holler, and installation was courtesy of David and Dawn Kelsch.

North Central College provided the perfect setting for *College, Community and Country* (15) at its Championship Plaza. Alums Al Benedetti, Bill Warden, and Dick Wehrli brought the project to us and funded it in part. Larry Gregory provided and assisted in its remarkable lighting.

Another use of city property gave *Cars of the Century* (16) a place to highlight early city car dealerships at the Van Buren Parking Deck, using stained glass donated by Ed Hoy International. Car dealers Bob Van Iten, Norm Zienty, and Neil Gerald were responsible for historical input and financial support.

2002: The "Video Professor," John W. Scherer, wanted to recognize his family heritage and donated not one, but two sculptures: *A Lifetime Together* (17) and *Be the Best That You Can Be* (18) in honor of his parents, William and Jane Latshaw Scherer. He endowed two annual scholarships in their names to Naperville Central High School. School administrators Dr. Donald E. Weber and Dr. Mary Ann Bobosky introduced Mr. Scherer to Century Walk.

After Dee Pasternak brought attention to the deteriorating condition of the 1926 doughboy, a "Save Our Doughboy" committee was formed consisting of Terry Jelinek, Ron Ory, Terry Ahearn, Bud Boecker, Judie Caribeaux, Wayne Fischer, Jim Healy, Steve Hyett, Sue Omanson, Frank Osterland, Stephanie Penick, Mayor A. George Pradel, Mike Rechenmacher, Chet Rybicki, Robert Schillerstrom, and Jack Schiffler. American Legion Post 43 and VFW Post 3873 joined together to support the renovation and secure donations of all denominations from hundreds of citizens. The Naperville Park District coordinated the project and rekindled *Spirit of the American Doughboy* (19).

CANDO (Central Area Naperville Development Organization) donated the *Yes We Can!* (20) sculpture they had commissioned in 1995, and Century Walk enhanced it with a plaque, granite benches, and a pedestal gratuitously designed by architect George Olson, one of several donations of his professional services.

2003: After thoroughly researching concepts and artists before making our final selection, we dedicated *Lean on US* (21) as part of the Commander Dan Shanower/ September 11 Memorial. Architects Peter Crawford, Richard Fawell, and Joe Drendel designed this many-faceted artistic tribute. Charles Johanns chaired a memorial committee of the following volunteers: Frank Allston, Craig Bloomquist, Dr. Mary Ann Bobosky, Lewis Breese, Joseph Dittmar, Gene Drendel, Dr. Richard Eastman, Dottie Farrell, the Honorable Harris Fawell, Ruth Fawell, Wayne Fischer, Gloria Johanns, Barbara Knuckles, Terese Krisch, Mayor A. George Pradel, Jon Shanower, Floyd Thompson, and Kenneth Wehrli.

Symbiotic Sojourn (22) saw Dwight and Ruth Yackley again take the lead in the expansion of Century Walk by substantially financing a fountain sculpture at Main Street Promenade highlighting Naperville's early prominence in the recycling era.

Century Walk Corporation
Board of Directors' Acknowledgments (Continued)

2004: The Board took a break from creating art in order to focus on raising finances. Scott Kolbe of Icon Digital Design designed an ad for Century Walk entitled "Preserve Your Face in Naperville's History" that encouraged 50 individuals to purchase a portrait of a family member or friend to be painted in *The Great Concerto* mural.

2005: Celebrating Rotary International's 100th birthday, the Rotary Club of Naperville conceived and partially funded the sculpture *Two in a Million* (23), honoring Walter (a former club president) and Grace Fredenhagen, at the site of his company's former headquarters. Again the Riverwalk Commission provided a perfect setting, and architect George Olson placed the couple where they could forever enjoy their treasures.

Nostalgia reigns in *The Way We Were* (24) on the north wall of the building owned by the estate of Jean A. Roberts. This look to the past was jump-started by Joan Hennessy, who selected the local artists and their topic and provided the initial funds to get it off the ground.

2006: Appropriately celebrating the Riverwalk's 25th anniversary was *Riverwalk Visionaries* (25), which was based on a photograph by Rick Hitchcock taken during the linear park's construction in 1981. Both the Moser and Rybicki families assisted the artist in creating the sculpture.

Volunteers Welcome (26) is a play on words welcoming visitors and was made possible by property owner Jim Kubal who "volunteered" his building's north face.

Kudos again to the City of Naperville for providing the large canvas for *The Great Concerto* (27) mural and the fifty-some individual portrait sponsors, especially the First National Bank of Naperville for placing the city's last four mayors in the portrait.

The Gene Darfler and Al Rubin families joined with Al Benedetti, Bill Warden, and Dick Wehrli in promoting and contributing to honor five Naperville WWII medal awardees and others who have served our country at *Veterans' Valor* (28). The American Legion Post 43 and Judd Kendall Post 3873 added the flagpole, and Naperville Concrete, Inc. supplied the base for the military heroes.

2007: Rounding out Phase I's 30 pieces are two works of art located a block apart just north of downtown on Washington Street. The first is *Parting the Prairie* (29), our kinetic sculpture at the DuPage Children's Museum, which is headed by Sue Broad.

The second, *Officer Friendly* (30), is located at Washington Junior High School where Bob Ross serves as principal. Superintendent Don Weber had previously secured a placement of our art on this school property, and the students voted and selected the topic as being most appropriate.

Our third art piece dedicated in 2007 was our first in Phase II, *The Cat in the Hat* (31). We were introduced to the project by Collette and Raymond Ruopp, proprietors of Framed Expressions Gallery who partially funded it. Brad McGuire, president of Jackson Storage, Inc., assisted in placing the sculpture. Tim Cardella, special services supervisor of Naperville's Public Works Department, oversaw the sculpture's storage prior to installation. Superintendent Dr. Alan Leis added to the dedication with a donation and by wearing his own "Cat" inspired striped hat.

2008: Once again the Board took a break from creating art and focused on raising finances. To aid us in this endeavor, we were the beneficiary of a grant from the Rotary Club of Naperville/Sunrise that funded *Moments in Time*, an excellent documentary of our work prepared by Executive Director Liz Spencer and the media team at Naperville Community Television Channel 17. Previously we were part of NCTV's "An Alice Neumann Special," which was recorded on August 5, 2000.

Century Walk Corporation
Board of Directors' Acknowledgments (Continued)

2009: Back-to-back Dr. Seuss sculptures resulted with the addition of *Green Eggs and Ham* (32) to our outdoor collection. The Chase Group, Inc. donated a portion of the purchase price and once again the Naperville Public Library, headed by Executive Director Donna Dziedzic, donated the land and cooperated in every facet of bringing the art to their 95th Street Library campus. This was our first piece to be located outside the immediate downtown vicinity.

Like *Green Eggs and Ham*, the sculpture *Mr. & Mrs. Naperville* (33) made its debut this year although it had been contracted for in 2008. This required great coordination and cooperation between Century Walk and the City of Naperville, Naperville Park District, Riverwalk Commission, and the Millennium Carillon Foundation. Jan Erickson, Chuck Pompano, and John Colucci, respectively, were most helpful in this regard. Greg Sagen, of Signature Design Group, Inc., saw to it that this art became a reality with a minimum of problems. Paul Lehman assisted the artist with information and pictures concerning the Mosers. Elenita Librojo, the Mosers' caretaker, gave an eloquent narrative of their kindness and generosity at the dedication.

Our northern-most location, the Naperville Fine Arts Center and Gallery, provides the wall for *World's Greatest Artists* (34). How could the Century Walk, which screams public art and history, be complete without capturing historically renowned artists? The art league's executive director, Debbie Venezia, was the glue that smoothly brought together venue, topic, and artists as we partnered with the Naperville Art League one more time for the sake of public art.

2010: Our signature piece, *Dick Tracy* (35), truly depicts the far-reaching aspects of public art as we combined an international icon with local roots. Tribune Media Services, Inc. licensed the sculpture. Chester Gould's family, consisting of his daughter, Jean O'Connell, and his grandchildren, Tracy O'Connell and Sue Sanders, donated funds, together with Marquette Properties, Inc., for its installation.

As in past years the artwork's formal dedication was followed by a reception for the public. The Naperville Municipal Center was the site for the many guests attending. Other receptions or presentations have been held in a myriad of locations and/or sponsored by very generous donors, including: Barnes & Noble, Catch 35, DuPage Children's Museum, Frederich-Jones Funeral Home, Carzz Grilleria, Holiday Inn Select (under three different managers – Paul Leisner, Mark Zettl, and Dennis Igoe), Jimmy's Brickhouse, Joan Hennessy, The Lantern, Lou Malnati's, Main Street Promenade, Naperville Art League, Naperville Central High School, Naperville Park District Rubin Center, the Naperville/Lisle Hilton, the Naperville Public Library, Sullivan's Steakhouse, and Washington Junior High School.

We would be remiss not to call the reader's attention to our state-of-the-art interactive Web site, **www.centurywalk.org**, created by 4-Next, Inc. proprietors Melanie and Chris Pusateri, assisted by board member Mindie Loebach. Now you will be able to take a virtual Century Walk tour and purchase gift items without leaving your computer!

Back to the Future – Our 501 (c)(3) not for profit corporation was chartered May 20, 1996, in Illinois and has been overseen by a board of directors consisting of Napervillians serving terms of varying lengths. We thank those presently serving* and others for their dedicated and valued contributions to our promotion of public art: Jim Bergeron, Brand Bobosky*, Bill Brittain, Fernando Castrejon, Kathy Channell*, Jini Clare, Jean Clark, Steve Coates*, Jonathon Croll, Glen Ekey, Roy Grundy*, Bart Gunderson, Peggy Halik, Meredith Harbour, Rita Harvard, John T. Higgins*, Rick Hitchcock, Sharon Hoogendoorn, Joe Hudetz, Steve Hyde, Steve Hyett*, Raye Isenberg, Susan Koranda, Michael S. Krol, Jill Lejsek, Mindie Loebach*, Sue McCarthy*, Julie McCutcheon, Dee Pasternak, Stephanie Penick, Pat Phillips*, Debbie Ridgon*, Shannon Greene Robb*, Pat Schmitt*, Joe Schultz, Drew Scott, Chuck Seidel, Willard Smith*, Mike Trippiedi, Don Weber*, Bettye Wehrli*, and Fran Wilson.

We fully intend to keep the faith as we move further into the twenty-first century with more exciting and meaningful public art throughout Naperville as we pursue **"Art Imitating History!"**

Art: *A vision of the soul*

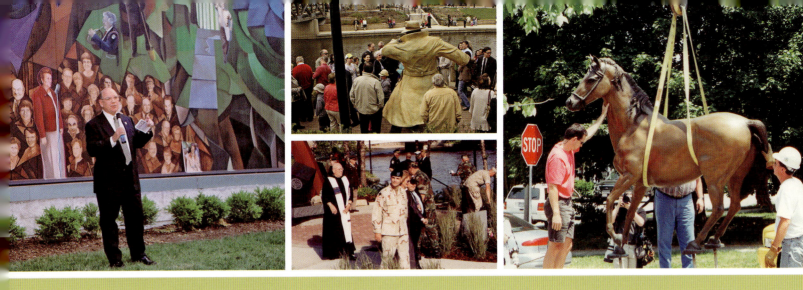

that transcends mortality.

~ Author Unknown

References & Resources

Information for this book was gleaned from my 12 years serving on the Century Walk Board, from interviews I conducted with artists and community leaders, and from numerous publications and other resources. Research was done primarily through the newspapers, magazines, Internet sites, and interviews listed below. I encourage anyone interested in learning more about the artworks, artists, or local history to use these resources to begin their exploration of this local treasure. The Century Walk Board and I would like to thank the local media, reporters, and photographers for their deep interest and coverage of this unique public art project from its inception. Their support has been invaluable. ~ *Jini Clare*

Introduction

Author's interview with W. Brand Bobosky, May 1, 2008.

Christiansen, Karri E. "Century Walk plan touted as legacy for the future." *Naperville Sun*, August 30, 1995.

Meisler, Stanley. "Take a look at a town that wouldn't lie down and die." *Smithsonian Magazine*, May 1994: 54-63.

Rackl, Lorilyn. "Making a pitch for paint." *Daily Herald*, January 26, 1996.

Zimmerman, Pucky. "Century Walk plan wins hotel tax hike approval." *Naperville Sun*, March 29, 1996.

Works of Art/Artists

A City in Transit

Author's interview with Hector Duarte, October 22, 2009.

Author's interview with Mariah de Forest, August 2, 2009.

www.hectorduarte.com

A Lifetime Together and *Be the Best That You Can Be*

Author's interview with Emanuel Martinez, August 6, 2008.

Author's interview with John Scherer, August 6, 2008.

Millen, Kathy. "A legacy in bronze: Scherer family sculptures are newest additions to Century Walk." *Naperville Sun*, November 8, 2002.

Museo de Las Americas. *Emanuel Martinez: A Retrospective*. Edited by Teddy Dewalt. Morrison, CO: Emanuel Publishing, 1995.

Stevens, Susan. "Software tycoon to give Naperville special gifts." *Daily Herald*, October 30, 2002.

Towsley, Genevieve. *A View of Historic Naperville*. Naperville, IL: The Naperville Sun, Inc., 1990.

www.emanuelmartinez.com

Cars of the Century

Author's interview with Sheri Law, October 28, 2009.

Corvette salesman. Bill Kay Chevrolet, Lisle, IL.

Research specialist. Benson Ford Research Center, The Henry Ford, Dearborn, MI.

College, Community and Country

Author's interview with Shirley McWorter-Moss, October 21, 2009.

Boutelle Tracy. "Statue immortalizes NCC football great." *Daily Herald*, October 21, 2001.

Heilman, Herbert. "To honor him and benefit others." *Moose Magazine*, June 1949:20, 26.

Millen, Kathy. "Remembering a hero." *Naperville Sun*, October 19, 2001.

Mooseheart Child City and School records.

North Central College Homecoming Program, October 19, 2001.

St. Clair, Stacy. "Statue to honor NCC football legend." *Daily Herald*, October 18, 2001.

www.mossstudios.com

Dick Tracy

Author's interview with Dick Locher, August 3, 2009.

Author's interview with Donald L. Reed, August 27, 2009.

www.dicktracymuseum.com

Genevieve

Author's interview with Pamela Carpenter, July 27, 2009.

Carpenter, Pamela S. Various documents, including "Artist Statement," "Commitment to Historical Content," and "Artistic Experience," 1998.

Farrell, Donna M. "An Old Friend to Take Her Place on Century Walk." *Naperville Sun*, February 24, 1999.

Millen, Kathy. "Art for the Masses." *Naperville Sun*, June 16, 1999.

Millen, Kathy. "A Storied Life." *Naperville Sun*, July 5, 2007.

McMahon, Jeanette. "Molding a Career Out of Bronze." *Daily Herald*, May 12, 1999, Wheaton, Glen Ellyn edition.

McMahon, Jeanette. "Naperville historian will be immortalized." *Daily Herald*, May 12, 1999.

Moy, Caryl Towsley. *Naperville's Genevieve: A Daughter's Memoir*. Bloomington, IN: Author House, 2008.

Pohl, Laura Zahn. "Historian to Live On in Bronze Sculpture." *Chicago Tribune*, May 20, 1999.

Golden Rule Days

Author's interview with Kristin Guill, April 3, 2009.

Millen, Kathy. "Golden-rule days: Sculpture to honor teacher's legacy." *Naperville Sun*, October 1, 2000.

Piccininni, Ann. "Newest artwork for Century Walk dedicated to teachers, Golden Rule." *Daily Herald*, November 5, 2000.

Stevens, Susan. "Longtime teacher's influence still felt." *Daily Herald*, November 5, 2000.

Growth and Change
Author's interview with Jack Holme, October 2, 2008.

Heartland Harvest
Author's interview with Kathleen Farrell, November 9, 2009.

Author's interview with Kathleen Scarboro, November 9, 2009.

www.fcpaonline.org

www.kathleenscarboro.fr

Horse Market Days
Allen, Kari. "Capturing a Moment in Time." *Daily Herald*, November 18, 1999.

Author's interview with Pamela Carpenter, July 27, 2009.

Author's interview with Robert Buono, July 21, 2009.

Author's interview with Torsten Muehl, July 22, 2009.

Millen, Kathy. "Pulling history closer." *Naperville Sun*, June 29, 2001.

Millen, Kathy. "Unveiling the past." *Naperville Sun*, November 19, 1999.

"Monthly horse market." *Naperville Clarion*, April 22, 1885.

"Public horse market." *Naperville Clarion*, May 27, 1885.

Stevens, Susan. "New statue a snapshot in time." *Daily Herald*, June 29, 2001.

Stevens, Susan. "Newest sculpture at Century Walk shows town's past." *Daily Herald*, June 23, 2001.

Wehrli, Joyce Elizabeth. *We Are Family: History of the Pre-Emption House and the Gertrude Hiltenbrand-Wehrli Family*. Naperville, IL, 1993.

www.tuttibuonofinearts.com

Lean on US
Author's interview with Bill Cooper, November 20, 2009.

McCammon, Sarah. "Freedom isn't free: Naperville dedicates sculpture, garden to legacy of fallen heroes." *Daily Herald*, September 11, 2003.

Millen, Kathy. "Designs on history: Committee hires artist to create memorial sculpture." *Naperville Sun*, December 8, 2002.

Shanower, Dan. "Freedom isn't free." From *Proceedings*, U.S. Naval Institute magazine, 1997. (Reprinted in *Daily Herald*, September 11, 2003).

Stevens, Susan. "Artist leaves no stone unturned for sculpture." *Daily Herald*, September 11, 2003.

Man's Search for Knowledge through the Ages
Author's interview with Mara Smith, October 6, 2009.

Maggiesmetawatershed.blogspot.com. "Meta Watershed: Mara Smith bringing ancient arts alive" (accessed March 5, 2008).

Nichols Library. "Smith brick wall sculpture donated by Hamer families." News release, April 15, 1987.

Rank, Pam. "Ancient art comes to life under sculptor's hands." *Naperville Sun*, December 17, 1986.

www.marasmith.com

Mr. and Mrs. Naperville
Author's interview with Barton Gunderson, May 3, 2009.

Ebner, Michael H. "Harold Moser's Naperville." Illinois Periodicals Online (IPO) Project, Northern Illinois University Libraries, 1999.

Griffin, Jake. "Mr. Naperville: City's premier developer, philanthropist was the host of the town." *Daily Herald*, April 27, 2009.

Towsley, Genevieve. *A View of Historic Naperville*. Naperville, IL: The Naperville Sun, Inc., 1990.

Naperville
Author's interview with Gregg LeFevre, September 30, 2009.

Towsley, Genevieve. "The Grapevine: Naper's history in bronze; this map's made for walkin'." *Naperville Sun*, November 5, 1986.

Naperville's Own
Author's interview with S. Michael Re, October 5, 2009.

S. Michael Re. "Artist's Statement."

Officer Friendly
Author's interview with A. George Pradel, November 25, 2008.

Author's interview with Sarah Furst, November 10, 2009.

Parting the Prairie
Author's interview with Christine Rojek, November 4, 2009.

Ogg, Bryan, research associate. Naper Settlement.

Rojek, Christine. Various documents.

www.christinerojek.com

References & Resources
(Continued)

Pillars of the Community

Author's interview with Dodie Mondero, September 1, 2009.

Harvard, Rita. Notes describing historical highlights of "Three Century Walk Murals at Sullivan's Restaurant." July 18, 2001.

Millen, Kathy. "Naperville's Who's Who" *Naperville Sun*, May 16, 2001.

Stevens, Susan. "Naperville's past captured in art mural." *Daily Herald*, May 27, 2001.

Stevens, Susan. "Picturing the past." *Daily Herald*, June 6, 2000.

Towsley, Genevieve. *A View of Historic Naperville*. Naperville, IL: The Naperville Sun, Inc., 1990.

www.napersettlement.org/history/kroehler_manufacturing_company.htm

The Printed Word

Author's interview with Timm Etters, July 20, 2009.

Towsley, Genevieve. *A View of Historic Naperville*. Naperville, IL: The Naperville Sun, Inc., 1990.

www.timmetters.com

Reading Children

AskArt.com: Dennis V. Smith.

Author's interview with Dennis Smith, October 23, 2009.

Author's interview with Doris Wood, September 21, 2009.

Millen, Kathy. "Sculpture carves its place in art exhibit." *Naperville Sun*, August 11, 1999.

Remes, Shirley. "Sculpture will enrich library collection." *Naperville City Star*, 1998.

Wikipedia: Dennis Smith (Sculptor).

www.smithsculpture.com

River of Life

Barrett, Kevin. "Naperville mosaic a work in progress for Century Walk." *Daily Herald,* April 28, 1999.

Bicksler, Linda. "Chipping in: Pupils help create latest Century Walk project." *Naperville Sun*, May 7, 1999.

Dell'Angela, Tracy. "Students leave their mark on Naperville." *Chicago Tribune*, May 6, 1999, Naperville edition, section 2.

Lelugas, Jane. "Patchwork project." *Naperville Sun*, September 23, 1998.

Minor, Ray. "Children take center stage on Naperville Century Walk." *Daily Herald*, February 27, 1998.

Ringgold, Faith, Linda Freeman, and Nancy Roucher. *Talking to Faith Ringgold*. New York, Crown Publishers, 1996.

Slack, Stacy. Various letters and project descriptions.

Stevens, Susan. "Impressions of life in Naperville." *Daily Herald*, May 29, 1999.

River Reveries

Author's interview with Jennifer Hereth, September 9, 2009.

Christiansen, Karrie. "Public can take first Century Walk on Sunday." *Naperville Sun*, November 1, 1996.

Culloton, Dan. "Great art takes time." *Daily Herald*, July 14, 1997.

Rackl, Lorilyn. "Public art to depict area's history, culture." *Daily Herald*, June 21, 1996.

www.napersettlement.org/history/kroehler_manufacturing_company.htm

Riverwalk Visionaries

Author's interview with Kathleen Farrell, November 9, 2009.

Clare, Jini Leeds. *Naperville's Riverwalk: Where History and Community Flow Together*. Naperville, IL, Clare Communications, 2006.

Hooker, Sara. "Sculpture captures spirit of Riverwalk." *Daily Herald*, May 2, 2006.

Penick, Stephanie. "Giving back for the future has long been the vision of Naperville." *Positively Naperville*, May 2006.

Spirit of the American Doughboy

Author's interview with Ron Ory, December 11, 2008.

Goldsmith, Earl D (with portions by Les Kopel). "Ernest Moore Viquesney." *The E. M. Viquesney Spirit of the American Doughboy Database*. http://doughboysearcher.tripod.com/id5.html, (accessed December 3, 2009).

Goldsmith, Earl D. "So Closes the Book, the Story Ends." *The E. M. Viquesney Spirit of the American Doughboy Database*. http://doughboysearcher.tripod.com/id5.html, (accessed December 3, 2009).

Goldsmith, Earl D. (With portions by Les Kopel). "The Spirit of the American Doughboy." *The E. M. Viquesney Spirit of the American Doughboy Database*. http://doughboysearcher.tripod.com/id5.html, (accessed December 3, 2009).

Naperville Park District. *The Spirit of the American Doughboy: Restoring a Naperville Treasure in Burlington Square*. 2003.

Owen County Public Library, Spencer, IN. Numerous research documents provided by Laura Wilkerson, genealogy specialist.

Viquesney, E. M. *The Artist's Story – How "The Spirit of the American Doughboy" Was Conceived*. American Doughboy Studios, Spencer, IN (date unknown).

Symbiotic Sojourn

Author's interview with Jeff Adams, September 22, 2008.

Boerema, Amy. "Praising the art of recycling." *Daily Herald*, November 3, 2003.

Sun staff. "Former resident got city recycling." *Naperville Sun*, March 31, 2002.

West, Tim. "Barbara Sielaff made a difference here." *Naperville Sun*, March 31, 2002.

www.inbronze.com

The Cat in the Hat and Green Eggs and Ham

Author's interview with Bill Dreyer, artist manager/curator, The Chase Group, LLC, December 15, 2009.

The Art of Dr. Seuss: A Retrospective on the Artistic Talent of Theodor Seuss Geisel. Published with special arrangement with The Chase Group, LLC. New York: Random House, 2002.

Dr. Seuss Enterprises. *The Art of Dr. Seuss: The Secret Art Collection*. New York: Random House, 1995.

San Diego Museum of Art. *The Art of Dr. Seuss: The Illustration Art and Archive Collections*. New York: Random House, 1986.

The Great Concerto

Author's interview with Barton Gunderson, July 23, 2008.

Foutz, Colt. "Faces in the crowd." *Naperville Sun*, September 27, 2005.

The Way We Were

Author's interview with Liza Netzley-Hopkins, July 16, 2009.

Author's interview with Marianne Lisson Kuhn, July 18, 2009.

Griffin, Jake. "Murals open nostalgia floodgates." *Daily Herald*, October 20, 2005.

Ogg, Bryan, research associate. Naper Settlement.

West, Tim. "Newest Century Walk mural a time machine." *Naperville Sun*, October 30, 2005.

Two in a Million

Author's interview with Rita Harvard, October 2, 2008.

Clare, Jini Leeds. *Naperville's Riverwalk: Where History and Community Flow Together*. Naperville, IL: Clare Communications, 2006.

Veterans' Valor

Author's interview with Shirley McWorter-Moss, October 21, 2009.

Dedolph, Meg. "Veterans Day unveiling of Century Walk sculpture honors Naperville's heroes of WWII." *Naperville Sun*, November 12, 2006.

Editors. "Uncommon valor – Sculpture immortalizes five of Naperville's most decorated World War II heroes." *Daily Herald*, November 11, 2006.

Jenco, Melissa. "Naperville's heroes immortalized." *Daily Herald*, November 11, 2006.

Jenco, Melissa. "Star-studded salute." *Daily Herald*, November 2, 2006.

Lynch, James. "Naperville's brave band of brothers." *Naperville Sun*, November 10, 2006.

Penick, Stephanie. "41st President recognizes Veterans' Valor." *Positively Naperville*, February 2007.

Piccininni, Ann. "Naperville dedicates sculpture to veterans." *Daily Herald*, November 12, 2006.

Taylor, Jennifer. "Naperville honors sons of war." *Chicago Tribune*, November 10, 2006, Metro West section.

World's Greatest Artists

Author's interview with Marianne Lisson Kuhn, July 17, 2009.

Author's interview with Mike Venezia, August 7, 2009.

www.mikevenezia.com

Yes We Can!

Author's interview with Bettye Wehrli, December 9, 2008.

Author's interview with Larry Swanson, October 21, 2009.

Central Area Naperville Development Organization, "CAN/DO History." July 26, 2001.

Danada Sculpture Gardens Association, *The Sculpture Show & Sale at Cantigny Park*. 1994.

Meisch, Sarah. "Village earns honor as Art Friendly Community." *Press Publications*, October 19, 2007.

West, Tim. "Generations of Napervillians have shopped at Wehrli's." *Naperville Sun*, November 19, 2008.

Photo credit: Joe Clare

About the Author

Jini Leeds Clare was born and raised in Ann Arbor, Michigan, and graduated from the University of Michigan with a Bachelor of Arts in English and a Master of Arts in Special Education. The daughter of two very talented artists, she grew up with an appreciation for art, artists, and the various media they use. Clare worked as a writer and editor before moving to Naperville with her husband and daughters in the 1980s. She served as communications director for the Naperville Park District for several years and then founded Clare Communications, an award-winning marketing and public relations firm. The concept of Century Walk piqued her interest when it was first presented, and the author served on the organization's board of directors for 12 years.

Clare has published several books, including *The Naperville Area Handbook and Guide*, a coffee-table book entitled *Naperville: Reflections of Community*, and *Naperville's Riverwalk: Where History and Community Flow Together*.

Naperville's Own / The Printed Word / River Reveries / Heartla...
Man's Search for Knowledge through the Ages / Reading Children / Genevieve
/ College, Community and Country / Cars of the Century / A Lifetime Together
Lean on US / Symbiotic Sojourn / Two in a Million / The Way We Were / Rive
/ Parting the Prairie / Officer Friendly / The Cat in the Hat / Green Eggs